DigiTales

The Art of Telling
Digital Stories

DigiTales: The Art of Telling Digital Stories

Bernajean Porter
15228 Rainbow Drive
Sedalia, CO 80135
ph 303-647-2294 fax

info@digitales.us
www.digitales.us
www.bjpconsulting.com

Inspiration: Sabra Shay Rawlings
Cover and book design: Catherine Perry
Editor: Sara Armstrong

Printed in the United States of America.

ISBN 0-9670755-4-8-978

Dedicated to my niece, Sabra Shay, whose shining spirit and friendship continues to sprinkle love, delight and warmth into my life everyday. Her ongoing encouragement along with intermittent inspiration talks brought out the best in this book. Here's to the making of our own story quilt telling the tales of our travel adventures together.

It is an absolute joy to be her Auntie.

Introduction vii

Let StoryKeepers be Heard Far and Wide

Digital Storytelling Blends the Ancient with the New; Writing as Joy and Fun, A Planet Full of Personal Stories; The Power of Digital Storytelling; DigiTales StoryTelling Camps

Chapter 1 7

That Reminds Me of a Story That Needs to Be Told

Once Upon a Time . . . the Role of Storytelling; The Storyteller's Spirit Work; Stories as Entertainment; Stories as Living Memories; Stories as Understanding; Stories as Healing Work; Stories as Future Vision; Stories as Community Building

Chapter 2 27

Enchanting Stories with Digital Tools

Storytelling, the Oldest and Newest of Arts; From Oral Storytelling to Written Tales; Enter Silent Picture, Talkies and Television; And Now . . . Digital Media; Imaginations Take Flight; Digital Media Formats; Photo Essays to Movies; Manipulating Media; Digital Distribution

Chapter 3 43

Storying Around Builds Useful 21st Century Skills

Information: The Raw Material of Change; Preparing to Learn, Unlearn and Relearn; Storying Around and Around; Creativity and Inventive Thinking; Multiple Intelligences and Learning Styles; Visual Literacy; Technical Literacy; Effective Communication; Effective Digital Communication; Teaming and Collaboration; Project Management Mentality; Enduring Understanding

Chapter 4 75

Conjuring Up Story Ideas

Life is Full of Stories; Personal Stories: Creating Living Memories; Kinship Stories: Family Stories of Who We Are; Hyper-Interactive Stories: Group Stories of Diverse Paths and Endings; Personal Expression: Creating Visual Expressions of Thoughts and Feelings; Myths, Legends and Tales: Past, Present and Future; Informative or Expository Stories: Information Beyond Words; Persuasive Stories: Influencing and Impacting Others; Itza Wrap: Telling Digital Stories of Lessons Learned; Future Vision Stories: Imagining the Future NOW

Chapter 5 105

Stepping Through Making a Digital Story

Crafting a Digital Story; Overview of Four Phases of Digital StoryMaking; Overview of Seven Process Steps for StoryMaking; Choosing Your Story; Take Six: Elements of a Good Story; Step 1: Writing a Narrative Script; Step 2: Planning the Project; Step 3: Organizing Project Folders; Step 4: Making the VoiceOver; Step 5: Gathering and Preparing Media Resources; Step 6: Putting it ALL Together; Step 7: Applause! Applause!; Calling All DigiTales Camp Storytellers

Chapter 6 141

Poof! Creating a DigiTales Toolkit

Let's Go Shopping!; In the Beginning . . . You Need a Computer; Getting Ready Checklist; Functions, Functions, Functions; Hardware Functions Checklist; DigiTales Software Toolkits; Software Descriptions; Pre-production Software Functions; Production Software Functions; Post-production Software Functions; Distribution Software Functions

Chapter 7 164

Entering the Technical World of Digital Media

Learning, Learning, Learning!; Everyone is an Expert - Everyone is an Amateur; Doubling Awareness of What You Don't Know; Start with Being Copyright Savvy; Creating a VoiceOver; Scanning Images; Understanding Image Resolution; Getting Images from a Camera; Getting Images from the Web; Editing Images; Getting Music and Sounds from CDs; Making Customized Music and Sound; Getting Music and Sounds from the Internet; Editing Music and Sound Files

Chapter 8 197

Extra! Extra! Resources for Digital Storytelling

Lots of Carts for Your Storytelling Journey; Articles; The Art of Telling Digital Stories; Big Ideas to Ponder; Copyright Savvy Resources; Digital Storytelling Websites; Evaluating Digital Products; Filmmaking; Free Software Downloads; Fun Animation Stories; Future Vision Books; Getting the Writing Spirit; Good News Story Websites; Hyper-Adventure Websites; Information Literacy; Learning in the 21st Century; Learning Styles; New Science Books; Organizational Storytelling Websites; Organizational Storytelling Books; Storytelling Associations and Resources; Storytelling Books; Storytelling Websites; Technology Learning Resources; Technical Websites; Visual Literacy Resources

In Conclusion 211

Introduction

Let Storykeepers be Heard Far and Wide...

Digital Storytelling begins with the notion that in the not too distant future, sharing one's story through the multiple mediums of digital imagery, text, voice, sound, music, video and animation will be the principal hobby of the world's people.

~ Anonymous

Digital Storytelling Blends the Ancient with the New

Digital storytelling takes the ancient art of oral storytelling and engages a palette of technical tools to weave personal tales using images, graphics, music and sound mixed together with the author's own story voice. Digital storytelling is an emerging art form of personal expression enabling individuals and communities to reclaim their personal cultures while exploring their artistic creativity. While the heart and power of the digital story is shaping a personal story about self, family, ideas, or experiences, the technology tools also invite writers and artists to think and invent new types of communication outside the realm of traditional linear narratives. There is something about using images, voice and music to craft a story that makes a different kind of story magic. Every aspect of storytelling – structure, plot, character, pace, voice, timing, and setting – has the potential to be artistically morphed into new communication forms using digital tools.

My own experience with Joe Lambert, Director of the Center for Digital Storytelling, opened a whole new world for me personally and professionally. My work with writing, thinking, communication and community building has been the core of my life's work since time began for me as a contributor to the world. I had previously spent almost fifteen years coaching students to be good writers, thinkers and public speakers – taking risks, being connected to others. I helped them enter their writing in contests, created a school poetry magazine, started a citywide debate tournament, and even tried engaging them in making their own filmstrips with colored markers or using 8 mm video cameras to tell their stories. Getting kids to enthusiastically put their hearts and minds into communicating their personal thinking and creative expressions was an endless cheerleading job. That was pre-desktop technology tools era when we used bulky analog technologies without affordable editing devices for fine-tuning or publishing their work.

Deep in a wooded forest, each of us is creating a path; the path is the story of our decisions, our thoughts, our fears and our hopes.
www.callofstory.org

A human being is nothing but a story with a skin around it.

~ Fred Allen

Then I took a job as state technology consultant for the Department of Education in Colorado helping educators invent powerful things for kids to do with technology tools. Still, even with new tools, crafting a piece of writing as well as developing oral communication skills was seen as a special talent or profession, risk-taking was low and the experience of public sharing left many feeling vulnerable and judged. Even my work with Bay Area Writing Project in which teachers experience being writers and then become teachers of writing, clearly left many with the technical writing skills but not with much joy or thrill for writing or sharing their own thinking and own personal stories.

Writing as Joy and Fun

The only time I ever had groups enthusiastically write was the collaborative storytelling developed at the many future searches I conducted. Here teams of community members wrote their one-page scenarios or personal stories of an imagined future as if it were already happening. The common qualities of their collective stories were expected to shift and guide their present actions and decisions towards a preferred, shared future. Fun, joy and creativity could be felt in all of these public readings of written future visions.

Today, as a professional speaker and trainer, and seasoned writer, I have gained a comfortable but hardly joyful experience with the ability to tell and write stories. But the digital storytelling experience I had with Joe Lambert through The Center for Digital Storytelling brought not only joy but also utter enchantment with the personal story I developed with digital media. I found out that I knew the technologies but had not connected with the inner spirit that communicating with digital tools can inspire. I became fired up to merge all my past experiences and skills into what has become a labor of love and passion – to engage kids and every kid-at-heart in experiencing the enchantment of telling their own personal stories with digital tools.

A Planet Full of Personal Stories

"Personal" is a key word here. As the explosion of personal Websites over the last four years demonstrates, there's no shortage of human beings on the planet with stories to tell and the desire to express them. All these living memories — an endless archive of thousands of stories can now be brought to life through visuals and sounds allowing us to share the story of us across time and cultures in powerful ways. All our stories can now be easily shaped into electronic photo essays, movies, sound stories, or Web and video essays by anyone with access to a desktop computer. You don't need to be a gifted writer, a professional video producer or an expert technology user. The low cost and availability of digital desktop tools now enables everyone young and old, professional and amateur writers/artists alike to participate in the telling and distributing of their stories, to join in reviving and preserving the ancient art of personal storytelling in new ways. Some of these tales win a wide audience; others might be meaningful only to a handful of relatives or friends. People of all ages can now easily enjoy a range of digital tools to experience the art of telling and sharing their personal life stories with just a little bit of help.

Traditional storytellers worry that the novelty and technical fun of multimedia tools will divert and endanger the quality of the story. It is a realistic concern that new storytellers who begin as technology lovers and become interested in digital storytelling may indeed tend to focus on the technical aspects they know and enjoy rather than the rich heritage and art of storytelling. If there is no substantive story to tell, then expensive digital tools will certainly not provide enough decoration to give a strong emotional staying power. Anyone crafting or leading a storytelling experience will need to focus their thinking on developing a STORY first rather than technology. No amount of technology techniques will fix a poorly written or flat, impersonal story. When the digital storytelling is finished, you want your story to be remembered for its soul, not the bells and whistles.

Stories tell us of what we already knew and forgot, and remind us of what we haven't yet imagined.

~ Anne Watson

The Power of Digital Storytelling

Storytelling has many roles in humanity's ancient, modern and future communities. The power of storytelling is being rediscovered and revived at a time in our world that challenges us to redefine who we are, our connections with others, and our ability to make personal meaning of a fast paced, chaotic world. The lines are being blended between professional and novice storytellers. The digital tools from word processing to movie making are available to the common man, woman and child. This gives the power of storytelling to people from all walks of life to discover they each have a story that needs to be told and the tools enabling them to experience the joy of finding and sharing their personal voices.

A man is always a teller of tales, he lives surrounded by his stories and the stories of others.

- Jean-Paul Sartre

There have been a number of incredibly talented people who have already marked the journey for me as well as others now traveling this road. I am indebted to many I have already met (Joe Lambert, Emily Paulos, and Mark Stanley) and many I still hope to connect with. A wealth of contact information about their work is included in my chapter called *Chapter 8: Extra! Extra! Resources for Digital Storytelling.*

To be a person is to have a story to tell.

- Isak Dinesen

There are a multitude of educators, researchers, corporate leaders, organizational change consultants, healers, church leaders and artists who are blazing this new trail in admirable ways. I publicly thank each of them for their vision, inventiveness, influence and genius. I recently experienced a number of aha's during a museum tour in Barcelona of Salvador Dali's work. His experimentation with all kinds of media forms started with thinking outside of most people's boxes. No technical pun intended. But Dali saw film, color, objects, perspectives, and design as a gigantic playground. There are many pioneers experimenting with blending technology and art as a form of communication. I encourage you to gather and learn from their good work. I invite you to wonder how their work along with your own might open new territories of creativity, communication, expression, community and personal vitality in your own life.

DigiTales Storytelling Camps

I am now transforming my past work of increasing communication, thinking skills, community building and personal possibilities with digital tools into workshops and a range of experiences called **DigiTales**. **DigiTales Storytelling Camps** provide a unique experiential event meant to give paper-trained adults an in-depth and personal immersion with reading and writing their own multimedia communication. Beginning with story circles, then preparing written scripts, gathering media resources, and finally mastering the software tools, digital storytellers learn the seven steps of storymaking to create the first of many, many 3-5 minute digital stories. Their stories range from creating living memories using personal and family stories to a variation of other story forms including interactive stories, persuasive stories, healing stories, community stories and stories of the future. Through the DigiTales Storytelling Camp experiences, everyone re-discovers the joy of learning, working as community, and reconnecting with their creative talents. Regardless of whether you are experienced with the digital storytelling technology tools or the art of storytelling or not, working over a period of three days from start to finish builds community, confidence, and pride in creating a completed story as well as having the skills to continue making digital tales happily ever after. Every group that I have gathered together to create digital stories leaves me even more inspired to evolve and continue this adventure.

This book is part of that inspiration. *DigiTales: The Art of Telling Digital Stories* is meant to inspire digital storytelling for all ages not just the young-uns or specialized groups. It is my best hope that a new generation of storytellers will become **StoryKeepers;** that our personal experiences, contributions, hopes and journeys will be recaptured for generations to come in a rich, expressive digital art form. **StoryKeepers** all over the world are creating and exchanging an important collection of personal digital stories in ways that lift up the possibilities and spirits of our hearts and communities. These are the stories that need to be told.

There is a certain embarrassment about being a storyteller in these times when stories are considered not quite as satisfying as statements and statements not quite as satisfying as statistics; but in the long run, a people is known, not by its statements or its statistics, but by the stories it tells.

- Flannery O'Connor

In Conclusion

While there are many technical books on hardware and software as well as traditional storytelling books, there are few books written that blend the power of both. This book will remind readers of the power of their stories while inviting them to move beyond oral story swapping, photo albums, scrapbooking or storybooks into the magical medium of multimedia. It is meant to help beginning digital storytellers select and use digital toolkits as well as provide resources to enable them to take first steps in storytelling. **DigiTales** is a starting place of ideas, resources and inspiration for families, individuals, schools, organizations, corporations, churches and everyone else who is ready to discover the power and magic of merging the art of storytelling with the fun of using digital tools.

May we find many of you discovering your talent and enthusiasm as **DigiTale's StoryKeepers**! I look forward to sharing this enchanted journey of digital storytelling in your very near future. Like paintings, your digital stories will exist over time and be enjoyed long past their creation, influencing and touching many individuals you will likely never meet. May your digital stories be heard far and wide!

Life will go on as long as there is someone to sing, to dance, to tell stories and to listen.

~ Oren Lyons

Chapter 1

That Reminds Me of A Story That Needs to Be Told

All families, tribes, and societies need resolute storytellers to constantly encourage, inspire and guide their people in a positive moral manner.

~ Donald Hamilton

Once Upon a Time . . . the Role of Storytelling

There is nothing new about storytelling. Stories are as old as people and as important. The Greeks did it. Abraham Lincoln did it. Confucius, Jesus, Buddha, Mohammad all taught their followers about ideas and hope with stories. Minstrels shared their stories (and gossip) accompanied by music. Before written language, history and wisdom were passed from generation to generation through oral storytelling. Bards were historians, keepers of genealogies, poets, composers of heroic stories, teachers of wit and wisdom, and tellers of mirthful (gossipy) tales.

Throughout history, stories have played an important part in education and in the development of wisdom. In early times, storytelling was used to explain significant and often confusing events such as storms, tidal waves, lightning, and fire. Special types of stories about heroes and gods were used to bind individuals to common belief systems. Moral tales conveyed the first codes or laws that ensured the harmony, cooperation, and ultimately the success of early human populations.

Stories of parents make good children.

~ Punjabi proverb

Stories infuse life with purpose, worth, meaning and value. Undeniably, stories can motivate us, cause us to recall, ponder, and embrace new ideas. Stories keep us company, entertain us, teach us, and pass wisdom among us. Modern businesses are coming to know that their products are less important than their stories. Some already have found that when specialists in the art of conveying human emotions through stories are included in the product design process, the resulting products are better conceived and more easily marketable. Designers and engineers may abandon even the most ingenious technical enhancements, if those enhancements can't be integrated into a product's story. (Olofson, *Dream Society*)

We are all storytellers. There isn't a stronger connection between people than storytelling.

~ Jimmy Neil Smith

According to Roger C. Shank, founder of the Institute for Learning Sciences (artificial intelligence) at Northwestern University, stories are at the core of human intelligence. Even Aristotle, often considered to be the master of rea-son and thought, indicated that wisdom was necessarily interconnected with myth and stories. (Lankton and Lankton, *Tales of Enchantment*)

The Storyteller's Spirit Work

Very little happens in our lives without a storyteller at its source. Storytelling includes all types of family and community gossip, religious and secular teach-ing, philosophy, prose, poetry, history, religious beliefs, myths, traditions, val-ues and morals, propaganda, scientific writings, speeches, news, advertising, plays, movies, songs, and television stories. Storytellers are extremely power-ful people. They have the personal power to guide, motivate, inspire, and influence. And all of us are storytellers.

Storytelling has grown immensely in its scope and power to influence in recent years due to the amount of information being generated and the many media through which we receive it. We are constantly being bombarded by stories of good and bad, by our family, friends, corporations, and media. Angeles Arrien, cultural anthropologist, says her studies show that 80% of our news media stories are negative. Storytelling, both positive and negative, is one of the most powerful tools of humankind. We quite simply become the stories we tell each other. As the daily dose of negativity permeates our culture and beliefs, a misperception grows among us that the people of planet Earth are generally unkind, uncaring, dangerous and unsafe. The "bad" is so continuous-ly put in our faces by news breaking TV specials and other communication media that fear is hyped by more fear until listeners also become part of man-ifesting a "morphogenetic field" of fear.

Morphogenic fields are non-material, invisible and intangible connections between human beings, their interactions and the influence of their actions. They carry information only, not energy, and are available throughout time and space without any loss of intensity after they have been created. These

We need to tell someone else a story that describes our experience because the process of creating the story also creates the memory structure that contains the gist of the story for the rest of our lives.

~ Roger Shanks, Tell Me a Story.

The universe is made of stories, not atoms.

~ Muriel Rukeyser

fields act as a geometrical influence, shaping behavior. Morphogenic fields are built up through the accumulated behaviors of species' members upon each other and the Universe. (Sheldrake Drake, *A New Science of Life*). "Basically, morphogenic fields are fields of habit, and they've been set up through habits of thought, through habits of activity and through habits of speech. Most of our culture is habitual, I mean, most of our personal life, and most of our cultural life is habitual." (Margaret J. Wheatley, *Leadership and the New Science*.)

The media's ongoing negative stories appear to take over the real truth about the people who live in this world . . .that we are really basically a good people. So where are the stories of everyday heroes? Where are the stories about our acts of kindness? Where are the stories of courage, caring and thoughtfulness by our kids, our neighbors, and our world community? What stops us from having these endless stories of hope and good of mankind be the eighty percent of our world news? Only the speaking of our own voices!

While we will always enjoy professional storytellers, it is time for all of us to take responsibility for putting our own good and inspiring stories into each other's lives. All individuals, families, organizations and societies need resolute storytellers to constantly lift up our hearts, possibilities and naturally good and generous natures. We each need to claim our own power as modern day storytellers, to consciously and publicly fill and change our cultural "morphogenetic fields" with the hope and goodness in our families, schools, organizations and personal lives.

All storytellers, family peers, friends, church leaders, students, teachers, movie producers, authors, politicians, philosophers, historians, comedians and civic leaders have the responsibility to guide, motivate, inspire and influence our present and future citizens. There is no better way than to use the communication media, including digital stories posted on Websites, presented at offices, shared with families, or showcased at community gatherings, to tell and celebrate the good and real story of us. We all can meet the challenge of lifting up the hearts and spirits of our fellow man beginning one story at a time.

The destiny of the world is determined less by the battles that are lost and won than by the stories it loves and believes in.

~ Harold Goddard

Under Cherokee Law, stories were told only to other Cherokees. The myth keeper would have to invite the listener to hear a story. The listener(s) would have to be cleansed by the Shaman before hearing the story.

Stories as Entertainment

Down through the Middle Ages, life was very precarious. Individuals preyed on individuals, feudal lords on other feudal lords, clans against clans, kingdoms against kingdoms. No wonder common folk, lords, knights, squires, monks and ladies all valued the amusement and diversion of the itinerant troubadours who brought ribald tales into their lives. Their nimble tongues brought merriment and amusement to all with tales of adventure, court scandal, heroic ballads, and various versions of current events. (Ruth Sawyer, *The Way of the Storyteller.*) These professional storytellers earned their living because of their talent to command an audience's attention.

Today we still find ourselves drawn to stories as entertainment. Television, movies, and theater provide millions with a diversion from the hectic pace of our modern life. However, with the advent of affordable laptops, easy-to-use digital production tools now offer story-making merriment to everyone. We no longer need to rely only upon professional storytellers to create "entertainment" for us. Whether creating video short cuts, documentaries or digital stories, all of us can now step into a troubadour's life and become master storytellers for each other and ourselves.

Stories as Living Memories

The first stories to mold our lives come from families. Our personalities and values are profoundly shaped over time through the stories told in our families. The memorable stories of our lives and others in our family take on special importance because they are true, even if everyone tells a different version of the same event. These kinship stories are told at dinner tables and repeated again and again at a multitude of family gatherings. Family stories were generally passed on while finishing chores, planting gardens, taking trips, eating meals, and sharing daily time together.

At the height of laughter, the universe is flung into a kaleidoscope of new possibilities.

~ Jean Houston

A Russian teller of tales is called "veselye lyudi" literally translated as joyous people.

~ Anne Pellowski, The World of Storytelling

These tales are precious family heirlooms, a gift of each generation that preserves itself by remembering their stories and passing them on. Apparently we need a certain amount of family lore to maintain a strong sense of who we are, a sense of self. (Elizabeth Stone, *Black Sheep and Kissing Cousins*.) Michael Roemer intriguingly declares that we are addicted to stories because they confirm our place in society. Shaping and expressing true stories about our lives and those of the people we've known can connect us more vitally with others; develop our creativity; strengthen our humor, courage, and confidence; and render our lives more memorable. (Michael Roemer, *Telling Stories*.)

However, many families today are not only widely scattered geographically, but job opportunities, company transfers, divorces, activities, and increased time commitments leave only minimal connections within many family branches. Today we have less time and reasons to gather as often in most families except for the occasional weddings and funerals or other special events. The common, daily places and spaces that were so natural for spontaneous listening and sharing of family stories and values are less available to us than ever. Even families who live together but get caught up in fast-paced world of work and activities find they have less and less together time. Stories keep memories alive. Your life stories as well as your family's stories about the most memorable life experiences are worth preserving. It is now possible through digital media to make your personal stories come alive for generations to come. Not only the story itself is captured and preserved. But the art of weaving original photos with living artifacts of voice, scanned artifacts and music literally leaves a living legacy through time.

Stories as Understanding

People today are quite simply up to their eyeballs in information. The more people are buried in the mind-numbing avalanche of today's information, the greater the importance of stories in making sense of the endless pieces of data. While storytelling does not replace analytical thinking, good stories do provide

When one is a stranger to oneself then one is estranged from others too. If one is out of touch with oneself, then one cannot touch others.

~ Anne Morrow Lindbergh

Stories have to be told or they die, and when they die, we can't remember who we are or why we're here.

~ The Secret Life of Bees

an essential process for conveying information in an easily absorbed form. They can relate very abstract ideas, science, or unfamiliar concepts with symbolic or analogous forms. (Stephen Denning, *The Springboard.*)

Nathan Shedroff writes a sidebar commentary in Richard Wurman's *Information Anxiety* describing the path from data to understanding. Data involves research and gathering. Information involves presentation and organization of relationships in the data. Knowledge involves conversations, storytelling and integration. Understanding (wisdom) involves evaluation, interpretation and retrospection of what we deeply know. As we go from data to information, to knowledge and then to understanding, we need to move from an impersonal to a highly personal connection to the subject or topic. By telling thoughtful stories, we clarify our own thinking about what we have learned and share it with others. We are able through story to personalize our understanding in a profound way that sticks with us over time.

Storytelling is an appealing way to develop and transmit deep understanding of complex and dense information. Even though stories are generally considered to be non-factual, narrative accounts of an event or events can be both true as well as fictional. The difference between simply giving a factual example and telling a story is the added emotional content along with including sensory details in the telling. (Annette Simmons, *The Story Factor.*) The topic or events within the story therefore become more personal and intimate for both the storyteller and listener. Discovering the personal meanings of topics or events helps us create memory, meaning and understanding of the data and complexity in our lives. It is the act of telling our personal story of what we know and understand from an event or topic that provides a "sense-making" process enabling us to deal with a myriad of data details. The story-making process enables us to simplify complex information into a core essence of understanding. By making sense of a learning experience that is also shared with others in some way, the information learned becomes infused with meaning and values rather than being passed on as simply facts. (Yiannis Gabriel, *Storytelling in Organizations.*)

Our species thinks in metaphors and learns through stories.

~ Mary Catherine Bateson

Story is the vehicle we use to make sense of our lives.

~ Anne Watson

The scientific world-view has invaded our work and schools, pervasively devaluing subjective experience in favor of information as hard facts. Qualitative research is frequently considered frivolous compared to scientific methods of quantitative data. Walter Benjamin, author of *Iluminations*, argues that traditional knowing that was once accumulated through experience has recently been supplanted by scientific knowledge based on proven information and hard facts. It is common belief that serious information should appear in tables, graphs, numbers, or at least communicated in a serious scholarly language. It is not that one is better than the other kind of knowing. We need to value and balance both experience-based knowing with the official knowing through facts. Stories enable listeners, stakeholders, and learners to transform facts-as-information into facts-as-experience.

Stories are an old way of organizing knowledge. Stories are an especially important method of organizing complex information by giving us a container to make sense of facts and data. In a famous essay called *The Hedgehog and the Fox*, historical philosopher Isaiah Berlin compared Tolstoy's *War and Peace* with conventional "scientific" histories of the Napoleonic invasion of Russia. Those histories presented only a succession of events. Tolstoy, by contrast, wrote history as a novel, using storytelling to arrange the facts in a way that gave them meaning and long-lived memorableness. (Peter Schwartz, *The Art of the Long View.*)

Roger Shanks, known for his work in artificial intelligence, comments that "learning from one's own experiences depends upon being able to communicate our experiences as stories to others." Constructing stories about what is known and understood encompasses a set of essential skills. By using personal interpretation to find meaning and connections between ideas, the storyteller creates linkages that build understanding and thus the essence of knowledge to oneself and others. By using digital stories to tell someone else the story of our experience and learning, we deepen our own understanding as well as extend our ability to share our perspectives and insights with others.

Information is not knowledge. You can mass-produce raw data and incredible quantities of facts and figures. You cannot mass-produce knowledge, which is created by individual minds, drawing on individual experience, separating from the irrelevant, making value judgments.

~ The Cult of Information

Stories as Healing Work

Stories are models for behavior, thought, and feelings. They heal our spirits by re-enchanting the disenchanted, introducing wit and invention, laughter and tears into our hearts. Susan Baur, a psychotherapist, suggests that when we express our interpretation of the past we open up new paths for the future. Many psychoanalysts contend that listening to others tell personal stories of their trials and triumphs also helps us in recovering from our own traumatic experiences. (Susan Baur, *Confiding: A Psychotherapist and Her Patients Search for Stories to Live By.*)

"Telling one's troubles to a best friend or therapist may feel good, but we may need to worry about the long-range negative effects *(of telling these stories)* on our memories." (Roger Schanks, *Tell Me a Story.*) Schanks suggests we are the stories we like to tell and gradually become the stories we tell more often. By dwelling on whatever stories you choose to tell repeatedly, the memory functions of the brain are reinforced. Schanks therefore suggests that sometimes "the storytelling aspect of therapy (healing) might work better if it were completely reversed" by encouraging people to tell happy stories.

Many healers as well as trained therapists have found the power of stories to stimulate, inspire, and remind us of what we already know. The metaphoric structure of telling a story offers us a message in the form of parables, myths or tales of experience. At one level the metaphors expressed are "just stories" that are interesting and engaging, but at another level the symbols and "truths" offered stimulate thinking, experiences, and ideas for problem resolution. (Lankton, and Lankton, *Tales of Enchantment.*)

As we tell our stories in the world, we make choices of how we make meaning of the events and experiences that influence who we are. Creating and sharing your digital story of a personal challenge or obstacle in life, a defeat, a betrayal, a life threatening illness, or a loss offers an opportunity to heal this experience. In a digital story, as you weave the words, images and music

There is no agony like bearing an untold story inside of you.

~ Maya Angelou

In the process of . . . discovering our story, we restore those parts of ourselves that have been scattered, hidden, suppressed, denied, distorted, forbidden.

~ Deena Metzger

together to unfold the crisis or situation, you also strive to find the essence of meaning or value this experience has made for your life. Each image or piece of music selected becomes a metaphor to express experiences beyond words. Like the traditional fairytale, after the hero or heroine has conquered and resolved their situation, there is a moral or lesson learned that enriches their life. Unfolding the digital story of a personal challenge or obstacle along with identifying the "moral" of the story creates opportunities for individuals to transform their experiences in healing ways. The sharing of our digital stories with others gives us a chance to offer our own learning as a profound healing of the heart for others who may have had similar experiences.

Stories as Future Vision

The future is where you are going to spend the rest of your life. We can't change the past, although if we are smart, we can learn from it. Things happen in only one place – the present. However, this "space" of time is too slim to allow us much more than reaction. It is in the yet-to-be future where we have time to prepare for the today's of tomorrow. (Joel Barker, *Future Edge.*)

What are the personal and collective future images held in our schools, organizations and communities for the 21st Century? How positive or negative are the images of the stories we tell of the future? How shared and urgent are these future visions? In a world of action and bottom lines, how important are future visions to our lives? Buckminster Fuller, author, scientist, inventor, poet, and engineer, believed that the success of the human experiment on-board Spaceship Earth depends greatly upon individuals having access to tools which empower them to see the Big Picture (vision) and together take strategic action. The decisive challenge is to generate a critical mass of awareness, matched by cohesive effort, focused on implementing our option for success before it expires. Fuller worked in many ways towards his vision that humanity has an unprecedented option to succeed. (www.bfi.org)

Stories set the inner life into motion, and this is particularly important where the inner life is frightened, wedged, or cornered. They show us the way out, down or up back to our own real lives.

~ Clarissa Pinkola Estes

The best way to predict the future is to invent it.

~ Alan Kay

To tell stories is to change the world.

~ Brother Blue

Stories can conquer fear, you know. They can make the heart larger.

~ Ben Okri

Stories knit together the realities of past and future, of dreamed and intended moments.

~ Joan Halifax

The future doesn't just happen: people co-create it through their action – or inaction – today. The larger the critical mass of people involved and committed to their shared future, the more likely that morphogenic fields of actions and behavior can be collectively influenced and shaped towards a desired future. "Any student of the rise and fall of cultures cannot fail to be impressed by the role played in this historical succession by the image of the future. The rise and fall of images precedes or accompanies the rise and fall of cultures. Great accomplishments are always preceded by great visions. As long as a society's image is positive and flourishing, the flower of culture is in full bloom. Once the image begins to decay and lose its vitality, however, the culture does not long survive." (Fred Polak, *The Image of the Future*.)

No one knows exactly what will happen in the future. But by actively deciding how they will live and work in an imagined future, by making choices today, children, adults, and organizations can collectively decide on the sort of future that would be most desirable and then direct their energies to achieve it. "Our visions of the future are the most powerful motivators for human change." (Joel Barker, *The Future Edge*.) What change do you want for yourself, your family, schools, organizations and communities? That is a digital story that needs to be developed and told.

In a world of fast-paced change, individuals, families, churches, schools and other organizations are being challenged to continuously re-envision who they are and what they want to become in order to adapt successfully to the changes brought to their lives. Visions define values and goals and enable us to shape our future rather than just let things happen. Do you ever wonder how the world will be transformed in the next 50-100 years? Can you see it? Imagine it? Feel it? Influence it? For many, seeing and believing an imagined future is difficult when everyday reality is so demanding and consuming.

When asked the question of where you will be in 25 or more years, many children, adults and organizations see only a blank screen or perhaps even worse, hold cynical images that reflect today's realities rather than imagined future possibilities. Vision statements without stories have less energy to bring them to life because words alone cannot engage us on a personal level. Writing scenarios can be used as a process to create rich stories about the positive way(s) you envision the future unfolding. Scenarios are future visions crafted into stories of what we do want rather than what we fear. While scenarios can be used as problem solving or decision-making processes that incorporate anticipated trends and patterns, they also can be used as powerful stories that translate vision into everyday realities.

> You can and should shape your own future. Because, if you don't, someone else will surely do it for you.
>
> ~ Joel Barker

Assumptions for Futuring

- There are many possible futures — if this were not true, there would be little point in this type of exercise.
- Not all possible futures are equally probable
- Not all possible futures are equally desirable
- What is most desirable among the possibilities is not necessarily most probable in the absence of some concerted effort to make it so.
- We explore the myriad possibilities of the future in order to understand the various opportunities and challenges that may lie ahead and therefore focus our actions and choices on realizing our preferred future.

> Stories are the single most powerful weapon in a leader's arsenal.
>
> ~ Howard Gardner, Harvard University

Scenarios are not predictions but rather they are about perceiving futures that will guide present actions and decisions. (Peter Schwartz, *The Art of the Long View.*) Scenarios create an intentionally detailed "picture" of dreams, imagined successes, and best hopes. They make the imagined real enough to be possible, thus mobilizing large numbers of stakeholders into immediate action towards what they do want for their lives. I have personally led over a hundred community and organizational visioning processes using the scenario storytelling process. It never fails that these stories of the future are infused with fun, energy, serious values, and a sense of urgency.

Having moved from oral storytelling to written text, digital storytelling now enables individuals and community groups to craft highly engaging vignettes that unfold their imagined futures with multi-sensory details. Digital stories of future visions evoke strong, positive emotions of hope and possibility showing what it is vividly like when we get to our imagined "there." While paper stories are generally published to share with others, the uplifting future vision experience only reached the ears of the group that participated. However, using the magic of digital stories, large numbers of other individuals and groups can grasp the change, why it might be desirable, and feel emotionally attached to the vision through Web postings, presentations and other media distributions. Those who were not there are thus able through viewing digital stories to experience, share, feel and participate together in living the new vision into reality as well.

Stories as Community Building

Telling stories together about things that really matter has an extraordinary effect on people. Understanding your own story prepares you to understand the stories of others. Something magical happens when people make and share real-life stories together. Stories are considered our primary means of connecting with each other so even more magic is possible when these digital stories are distributed and related meaningfully to quite literally a world community through the World Wide Web. The magical power of releasing our own story in our local and global communities is its ability to create understandings, build positive relationships, and leverage shared values between people of different communities or cultures.

Traditionally, a community was generally homogeneous with its boundaries based on proximity. The neighborhood was mainly German, Irish, African-

Storytelling is the most powerful way to put ideas into the world today.

~ Robert McKee

Values are meaningless without stories to bring them to life and engage us on a personal level.

~ Doug Lipman, The Story Factor

American or Chinese. A business was mainly Jewish or Protestant. The neighborhood schools taught children from a common economic and often similar ethnic background. The local clubs were mainly one group or another. Now many communities and groups are experiencing an insurgence of unprecedented diversity in their memberships. Some school districts are dealing with have up to sixty-two (62) languages spoken by their students and at least as many cultural differences across their classrooms. Corporations are competing in a world economy as well as hiring employees from multiple countries to deliver services remotely that were once performed by local help.

Few communities today are homogenized. People young and old are finding themselves living, learning and working next to each other rather than with each other. Many have become lost in this increasing diversity by focusing on their mutual differences rather than our commonalities. "Disease of loneliness is most common today with 75% of the population not even knowing their neighbors." (Joel and Michelle Levey, *Renewing Spirit and Learning in Business.*)

What will replace the commonality that was once based in the shared sameness of ethnicity, religion, race or geographical proximity? Claire Gaudiani, author of *Wisdom Tradition*, proposes that it is being replaced by a growing need she calls "wisdom tradition." It is the work of developing commonly shared values as human beings that can exist across time, geography, and cultures. We often associate the term "capital" with purely economic ideas of profit, efficiency, and material wealth. Gaudiani challenges us to see the notion of "capital" in a larger context as something that adds value to the well-being of a community. She proposes that in a time of growing change and complexity, without wisdom capital and the values it sustains, we cannot have strong and healthy communities. Wisdom capital is the product of stories revealing values and shared experiences that are passed from generation to generation and from people to people.

Angeles Arrien, a cultural anthropologist, shared the following thoughts in her

We are the first generation bombarded with so many stories from so many authorities, none of which are our own. When saturated by so many points-of-view, we lose our own experiences and stories; we become people who are written on from the outside.

~ Sam Keen

The longer we listen to one another with real attention the more commonality we will find in all our lives.

~ Barbara Deming

If it had not been for storytelling, the black family would not have survived. It was the responsibility of the Uncle Remus types to transfer philosophies, attitudes, values, and advice, by way of storytelling using creatures in the woods as symbols.

~ Jackie Torrence

Winter 2003 Wisdom Tales workshop. Storytelling is one of the oldest arts of reopening our hearts and bringing us back to our humanity. She laughs as she exclaims, "the Great Spirit must have loved stories because he made so many people." Every person has a story to tell that is important for others to hear. Arrien builds on this idea of diversity by proclaiming that the wisdom tales of the world can provide opportunities for us at this time in history to understand how we can make wiser choices. She believes it is possibility in the next 50 years for us to move out of a power status, privileged, materialistic society into a wisdom society much like Claire Gaudiani proposes. What would it take to catalyze that? Arrien suggests that we band together to create a critical mass or a tipping point that would shift this power by reaching ordinary people's deepest, inherent values. I believe like Angeles Arrien that the human spirit wants to contribute, has an incredible generosity of spirit; and would if given a chance create a world as a better place. We can collectively start this process increasing hope for our world through sharing compelling stories – digital stories.

Today, communities boundaries based on shared values are becoming more common than geographical proximity. When stories are gathered as living memories from community groups, their intimate and authentic perspectives develop these shared values by finding common experiences, concerns or issues that bind them together. The unity of diverse groups within neighborhoods, churches, schools, businesses, organizations, cities or even nations who have been able to develop strong connected communities are not accidents or flukes. Sharing stories forges relationships and connections between families, neighbors, workers, learners and other human members. Real-life stories bring individuals a greater sense of intimacy with others and their own sense of self. Every culture is able to use story as a universal language to break barriers and misunderstandings that form empathic bonds between storytellers and their listeners.

Even in work places and organizations culture and values are passed on through story. The history of the organization, successes, challenges of the

Community Digital Storytelling Websites

Here are a few examples of community digital stories that demonstrate the power of holding events for ordinary people to experience the power of using technology for telling their own truths in their own voices.

Digital Story Bee – a free workshop designed to help women tell family stories while demystifying the technology behind the World Wide Web. They came together with a couple of family photographs and told stories in a circle a bit like an old quilting bee. The women shared stories about their grandmothers and then put them on the Web. (www.bubbe.com/dsb/index.html)

Capturing Wales – a national consortium including BBC wanted to use multimedia as a tool to educate, organize and celebrate the stories of people in the diverse towns, villages, and cities of Wales. The Center for Digital Storytelling was invited to help initiate a series of monthly workshops working with members of the public to help them create their own digital stories. (www.bbc.co.uk/wales/capture-wales/tg/community.shtml)

Community Histories by Youth in the Middle East (CHYME) - an initiative to increase understanding and connections among Middle East youth for cross-border community activities. Their personal stories share experiences and insights of living with the ongoing conflicts in the Middle East. (www.cctvcambridge.org/stream/qt/chyme)

Stories of Service - a national initiative dedicated to mobilizing young people to serve their communities by helping preserve the stories of our nation's veterans. (www.stories-of-service.org/theproject)

Third World Majority (TWM) - a new media training and production resource center run by a collective of young women of color and allies dedicated to developing new media practices that affect global justice and social change through grassroots political organizing. Their use of community digital storytelling workshops to assist people in telling their stories as three-to-five minute digital videos demonstrates the power of personal stories. (www.cultureisaweapon.org)

organization, are often defined through its story. Tom Peters, *In Search of Excellence*, wrote that in the workplace, it is all about reaching people's values through inspiration and motivation, which takes storytelling. Stories become a powerful and practical communication that reinforces values by creating a kind of glue that holds the community together, even at a distance. Cultural storytelling is a way of bonding people. These personal stories are able to touch hearts and connect us to the humanity of each other.

In Conclusion

All digital stories (personal, kinship, beyond words, future vision) are community stories that enable people to experience invaluable access to multiple community perspectives on important life issues as well as providing an important and powerful forum for communities to tell their own truths in their own voices. These digital stories are shaping social, historical, and political forces by building coalitions, advocacy alliances and an understanding of shared values across geographical and ethnic boundaries.

If we see ourselves as helpless victims, unable to change our world, we will keep finding and telling those kind of hopeless versions of ourselves. If on the other hand we see ourselves as capable and willing to participate in changing the world, we can through our stories enhance our own and other's ability and willingness to adopt a more positive outlook. By creating more positively oriented stories for ourselves, in due course we begin to act out these positive stories and so the world is changed by one action at a time.

It is possible that the accumulation of our personal stories whether oral, print or digital can indeed create the tipping point that changes our chaotic, fragmented world into a world community. Gladwell introduces the concept that ideas can be infectious, creating social epidemics. The success of any kind of social epidemic is dependent on but a few. (Malcolm Gladwell, *The Tipping Point.*) But with the use of the Internet, and other emerging forms of distribution, our digital stories can now provide an even stronger catalyst for creating communities of common concern and caring on a global scale. And those are the stories that need to be told.

The greatest revolution of our generation is the discovery that human beings, by changing the inner attitudes of their minds (with stories), can change the outer aspects of their lives.

~ William James

Chapter 2

Enchanting Stories with Digital Tools

A new technology does not wipe out what went before; it transforms and enhances it. When people started writing, they didn't quit talking.

~ Walter Ong

Storytelling, the Oldest and Newest of Arts

Since the beginning of time oral storytelling was an essential element in forging friendships, alliances, families and communities. Even though the technologies of print, film and now digital media have transformed storytelling in a multitude of ways, traditional oral storytelling is still experienced in homes, schools, churches, businesses and theaters today. After many years of a world emphasizing math, science, logic and bottom lines, storytelling is experiencing a resurgence in many forms. Even though we are enjoying many, many different storytelling forms, traditional oral storytelling still prevails as an important human experience in many cultures including our own. From primitive family storytellers to the early bards, troubadours and minstrels to formally trained professional storytellers, the art of telling stories has always belonged to the storyteller regardless of the medium. Their stories endure because of the personal artistry and style in sharing the heart and spirit of a tale.

Through the ages the art of storytelling has been shaped into many other forms, from written texts to expressing story through theater, comics, film, art and photographs. Storytellers have adapted and transformed the story form with each successive medium that has emerged. It took 2,000 years of writing before an alphabet was developed. It took a century and a half of printing before someone thought to print a novel or a newspaper. New communications technologies do not arrive upon the scene fully grown; they need time to develop the methods and forms that best exploit their potential. From campfires and castles to social and communal gatherings to books to the stage and silver screen and now . . . to the computer screen, storytelling has been shaped and reshaped by the inventiveness of users engaging with the new mediums.

A good story should have a beginning, a middle and an end . . . but not necessarily in that order.

~ Jean-Luc Godard.

From Oral Storytelling to Written Tales

Like Plato who expressed concern that moving from oral recitation to the written word compromised thinking and learning, many traditional oral storytellers feel their craft is being compromised by the new mediums.

Some people may feel that because written language is about words preserved on a printed page, the only difference between the written story and the oral story is the fact that one comes through our eyes and the other through our ears. But the nature of oral storytelling is not a simple transcription of the words. Donald Davis, author of *Telling Your Own Stories*, describes five languages used in telling stories to living groups of listeners:

1. Dialogue using words to engage readers in the story
2. Hand, face and body gestures that extend meaning to the words
3. Sound or tone of words spoken
4. Emotional attitude conveyed by the storyteller through eyes, posture, and face
5. Audience feedback which molds the pace and content of the story with their reactions

If we attempt to transcribe the unique qualities of oral stories into mere text, many more words are definitely needed to compensate for the gestures, sounds, pacing, and emotional attitude conveyed to live audiences. One distinct feature of oral storytelling entirely lost with written stories is the influence of the audience's feedback during the live storytelling. Their reactions make each telling a unique experience for both the teller and the listener. Unlike written language, oral storytelling is real-time based with the listener only receiving the information when the storyteller shares it.

Written language is captured in a medium that brings the advantage of letting the reader (listener) choose to reread, pause, savor, go back to review, look ahead or abandon the story. Written stories can also be enriched with intriguing illustrations, symbols, color and other visual devices. These text stories are available to readers when desired rather than only available when a storyteller is around.

Walter J. Ong in *Orality and Literacy: The Technologizing of the Word* makes an important observation about all cultures, including our own: we are all born into an oral culture first. Oral communication is our natural language and the impulse to tell stories a part of our genetic makeup. He outlines the intriguing kinds of changes cultures undergo as they move from oral to literate (with writing) societies. Ong further differentiates between languages that have a written form (hand written manuscripts) and those that have a printed form (books) in shaping the culture of people. The medium not only changes the story form but also influences cultures as well. We shape the medium but the medium also shapes us.

The average person spends about two hours per day reading at the rate of about 200 words per minute. www.balancetime.com/speedread.htm

Print verses Television

Michael Rosenblum, the President of NYT-TV, observes one of the primary differences between print and television is that "print has always enjoyed a rich environment that ranges from comic books to Shakespeare. The words have come from millions of writers with pens, and typewriters and word processors, and the best have risen to the surface. Television, on the other hand, has always flowed from the top down."

Milestones in Film History

65 B.C.E. The Roman poet Lucretius discovers a basic principle still used today in filmmaking, the persistence of vision. Persistence of vision means that when the human eye views an object under a bright light, the visual image of that object will persist for one tenth of a second after the light is turned off. Therefore, as each film frame appears, it does not fade out until the next frame appears.

1832 The Belgian scientist Joseph Antoine Ferdinand Plateau develops the phenakistoscope, the first device that allowed pictures to appear to move.

1877 The San Francisco photographer Eadward Muybridge is the first to photograph motion when he set up 24 still cameras along a racetrack. As a horse ran by the cameras, the horse would break strings that were hooked up to each camera's shutter. When a string broke, the shutter of that camera would open exposing the film.

1896 Edison presents the first public projected motion picture on a screen in the United States at Koster and Bial's Music Hall in New York City with his latest invention, the projecting kinetoscope.

1899 The French magician Georges Melies becomes the film industry's first artist by being the first to use movies to tell a story. Melies wrote, designed, directed, and acted in hundreds of his own fairy tales and science fiction flicks.

1903 The American director Edwin S. Porter releases his most important film, The Great Train Robbery, which was the first movie to use modern film techniques such as filming out of sequence for practical reasons and later editing the scenes into their proper order.

Enter Silent Pictures, Talkies and Television

The camera brought new opportunities and new changes to the art of story-telling. The first generation of cinema storytelling was silent pictures. The limitations of the silent form forced filmmakers to be imaginative and develop a visual language that enabled them to say with images what they could not convey with dialogues (words) or sounds. Directors, screenwriters, and actors perfected this visual language to communicate their stories.

By the time sound arrived in the late 1920's, many silent film directors and actors, including Charlie Chaplin and Alfred Hitchcock, not only felt it unnecessary but argued that the new technical feature of sound caused the art of cinema storytelling to suffer. Hitchcock is a director who began his career in the era of the silent movies and then went on to direct "talkies" as well as television shows. A 1929 British movie called *Blackmail* was filmed by Hitchcock as both a silent and a sound film. Viewing the two movies side-by-side makes an interesting case study of how different mediums influence the telling of the same story as Hitchcock had to modify his style of shooting and editing for the new film medium that included sound. But he continued his film career believing that dialogue and sound should remain secondary to the image in telling a story.

With the development of television and movies, many became concerned about the amount of time spent watching these new mediums compared to the time spent reading a good book. Today with the advancement of technologies like computer-generated graphics, the television and film industry continue to experiment and invent a multitude of new storytelling styles. There continue to be those who predict that books as we know them will soon disappear. The reaction to television, movies and computers is similar to Plato's fear of print. Many fear that intellect, culture and a way of life has become lost with people spending fewer than two (2) hours per day reading compared to an average of five (5) hours per day watching television. A national nonprofit organization called TV-Turnoff Network encourages chil-

The silent pictures were the purest form of cinema.

~ Alfred Hitchcock

A film is never really good unless the camera is an eye in the head of a poet.

~ Orson Welles

Who the hell wants to hear actors talk?

~ H.M. Warner, Warner Brothers, 1927.

dren and adults to watch much less television in order to promote healthier lives and communities. (www.tvturnoff.org/index.html) Like oral storytelling which still remains an important medium, reading also remains a significant part of our culture even though we are now choosing to make room in our time and thinking for the newer mediums.

And Now … Digital Media

Across a blank screen, a black and white photo of a young teenager fades into view with haunting piano music playing softly in the background. This is the dramatic opening of Amy's digital story. She has posted it on the Internet to share with other teens the dangers of leaving home to meet in person a man whom she first met online. As her 15 year-old voice begins her personal story, floating text rhythmically appears and fades out of view emphasizing key thoughts from her story "I didn't know," "I didn't think," "He said, 'I'll take care of you.'" Keyboard clicking is heard in the background of an image of a person sitting at a computer showing us the beginning of her dangerous choices. Shifting dissolving photographs of varied poses of Amy unfolds the story of why she was vulnerable and tempted to talk to a stranger online. The momentum builds as the visuals and voice weave together a scary tale of a young girl who could easily become a victim. Her message becomes emotionally evocative as the animation of an unknown man runs towards her photo. A police car photo with a siren slides into her story, stopping visually between her and the animated man. The sounds, animations, photos and her voice emphasize a scary, happy and safe ending for Amy. But she closes with a warning – a lesson learned: "You never know who that person (online) is and what he is capable of doing. I was lucky." This is a personal digital story called *Amy's Choices*. (www.netsmartz.com)

Amy's story casts a deeply moving spell using the art of digital media to engage her viewers, hopefully changing other teenager's choices about meeting online strangers. The time she spent reflecting and struggling with how to express and show her feelings with the events, and then finding the lesson learned from this experience, empowers her as well. Her electronic memoir shared on the Internet is now exposed to a world wide audience. *Amy's Choices* is just one example of hundreds of ordinary people spinning and sharing their tales with digital media.

Edwin Camacho's digital story...

Thanks to My Mother relates the challenge of raising a son as a single dad. It illuminates the wisdom Camacho receives from his own single mother's story of rearing five children. His tale has reverberated with many of his neighborhood's single parents, keeping many mothers from believing that only women face single parenthood. Mamie Marcus, (*The New Community Anthology: Digital Storytelling*)
(www.bos.frb.org/commdev/c&b/2003/fall/digital.pdf)

The storyteller's voice, considered the center and heart of every digital story, weaves together a tale with photos, images, artwork, video clips, and animation along with sound effects, transitions and music. These personal stories are a source of inspiration to the authors as well as viewers. Even though we may never have a chance to meet these storytellers in person, they share with us a brief peek into their souls and life events. Each story strives to document challenges, highlighting lessons learned, solutions, meaning and hope. The digital environment provides a unique opportunity to empower people of all ages to manipulate, combine and distribute their self-expressions as living stories that can be sent into the world and through time. Digital tools give all storytellers the ability to create special personal magic. Each completed story becomes an enchanted tale evoking pride and self-fulfillment in expressing a story that needed to be told.

Someday in the distant future, our grandchildren will spend hours in front of boxes with fires glowing within. May they have the wisdom to know the difference between light and knowledge.

~ Plato

Imaginations Take Flight

The gap between professional and amateur digital production has now become blurred giving new wings to the imaginations of everyone with access to a personal computer. The cost of creating a personal digital story to share with anyone anyplace has fallen so dramatically that the art of telling digital stories no longer belongs only to a specialized class of professionals. Owning the same artful tools as professional Hollywood directors gives everyone of all ages the opportunity to be creative and circulate their own media rich stories. It is a virtual playground stimulated by both our love of stories and years of enchantment with television shows and movies. We can now be our own stars – take our own film footage, scan anything into digital files, transform popular scrapbooks into family television shows with a magic flair.

Digital stories are now an affordable reality for anyone wanting to produce their own living memories. Bob Levine, author of *The little iDVD Book*, talks about anyone in the pre-desktop video era needing a pocketful of cash to create a video good enough to be shown on television. Levine states that renting a video-editing studio of "broadcast quality" ran from $100 to $1000 per hour. It cost $5000 to $10,000 to produce a single 30-second commercial. Today spending $2000 to $3000 on a computer that generally comes with specialized software starts a home studio. These affordable digital tools have been discovered and people are finding great fun and pleasure in expressing their imaginations. See *Chapter 6: Poof! Creating a DigiTales Toolkit* for detailed information on selecting hardware and software.

Digital Media Formats

Unique to digital storytelling is the personal ability to use any type and combination of media along with being able to distribute it far and wide. Examples of media formats that can be combined are graphic, motion graphic, video, animation, text, photo, audio, music, sound effects and special effects. Digital stories engage unique features of both content movement and user-controlled action. Nora Paul and Christina Fiebich outline five elements of digital stories along with documented research findings. (www.inms.umn.edu/elements) Paul and Fiebich describe with online examples three types of configurations for digital media: single, multiple and multimedia.

* Single media uses only primarily one medium to tell the story, such as text or video.
* Multiple media uses two or more types of media but as separate components of the story package without interweaving them, for example online news that have sidebar context information related to the story.
* Multimedia uses two or more media types woven together into a seamless presentation, such as text, audio, and video.

A new medium is never an addition to an old one, nor does it leave the old one in peace. It never ceases to oppress the older media until it finds new shapes and positions for them.

~ Marshall McLuhan

Distribution Formats for Story Sharing:

* Make your own DVD's to swap with others. Dress up your digital movie with all the features of blockbuster DVDs, including chapters, themes, menus and interactive features.
* Make your own VHS tapes ready for anyone to use at home, school, office.
* Save digital stories as QuickTime (QT) movies ready for presentations, emailing.
* Post your QuickTime (QT) digital movies to the Web to share with everyone!
* Take your digital movie with you on your PDA or cell phone if you have a compatible Bluetooth device. Who knows what stranger may be yearning to see your movie!

Photo Essays to Movies

Many first time digital tool users begin with photo essays. This is the sequencing of a series of pictures and then adding appropriate music to visually share an experience. While photo essays can be a very expressive art form, many often look like slide shows turned into movies. However by starting with the story script FIRST, the images, sound and special effects are then selected to shape a digital story making it more dynamic than a simple picture show.

Another type of still photo essay is changing the work of professional photojournalists by combining documentary photographs with ambient sounds and an audio recording of a subject's own narrative interpretation or sound-bite essay about the photo. Brian Storm, in his article "Made for the Medium," discusses a new focus at MSNBC.com that now plays to the unique strengths of digital medium by adding value to still images with in-depth, tightly edited audio/video components. The goal is to use new technology so effectively that it fades into the background as the story focuses on giving the reader an evocative experience about other people's experiences, feelings and place in historical or current events. Instead of photojournalists simply TAKING a picture, they can now GIVE their photo subjects and events a voice. The power of a subject's personal voice combined with artful photographs is worth experiencing. See examples in Storm's article at www.digitaljournalist.org/issue 0203/storm.htm or experience other examples at http://msnbc.com/ modules/theweekinpictures

Film-making is a collaborative process often requiring an 'army' of people to bring a final movie into reality. Writers, directors, cast, camera crew, sound crew, editors and producers are just a few of the roles that have to be filled. These are usually more tasks than any single individual would take upon themselves. The film topics range from fictional stories to biographies, public service messages, documentaries on topics that investigate critical issues of the day or 'short-takes' on creative topics. The movie is generally entirely constructed with video footage. After the story script is developed, shot lists are created to organize the shooting of the video clips or footage needed. There are thousands of details with shooting schedules, set decorations, lighting, casting, costumes, and props to name a few. It is an exciting experience to craft a professional quality film involving many more skills than the 'point and shoot' of many amateur uses of video.

While many users of digital media call film-making "digital stories," there are at least three distinct differences. First, digital stories use a range of multimedia (voice narration, animation, scanned memorabilia, or still images) and may not even include any video clips at all. Second, the personal telling of the story - the narrative voice that makes meaning out of the experience or information - is essential to all digital stories but may or may not be part of the visual expression of a good film. Third, the expectation for personal narrative makes the construction of a digital story more suited to individual projects than group projects. Each production decision reveals the individual's intimate connection with their topic. The author is living in the experience rather than 'telling about' a topic. A digital story shares knowledge and experience through the heart rather than the mind. This is an option but not a requirement for a good film.

Manipulating Media

In oral storytelling, the meaning of a story is manipulated by voice tone, pacing, gestures, and body language. In digital media, the meaning of the story being narrated can also be manipulated with images, color, text fonts, sound effects, music, transitions, animations, special effects, pacing, and image/video composites. We experience the phenomenon of media manipulation in news, mass marketing political, and public service stories.

Intentional manipulation of media influences or impacts the target audience(s) both verbally and non-verbally often sending subliminal thoughts into the unconscious. This manipulation can be used for good as well as for bad pur-

Do you realize if it weren't for Edison we'd be watching TV by candlelight?

~ Al Boliska

Number of years it took for each medium to reach 50 million people: Radio - 30 years; television - 13 years; Internet - 4 years; and Napster - 2 years.

~ Workshop quote by Chris Klein

poses. Making powerful digital stories can create an awareness of local or world community issues. The purpose of these stories aims to help us create a better world through such actions as getting people to vote, understanding child labor issues, developing compassion for neighbors or actively taking care of an endangered environment. See *The New Community Anthology: Digital Storytelling* www.bos.frb.org/commdev/c&b/2003/fall/digital.pdf See video examples of community building work at www.creativenarrations.net.

On the other hand, if consumers are not media savvy, if they have not experienced being "writers" of multimedia themselves, it is easy to become unconscious victims of media manipulation. Consider comparing and contrasting an online political video clip in which various media (color, sound, music, voice, text, and film speed) are manipulated to represent one version that would encourage voters to be FOR a candidate and a second version that encourages voters to be AGAINST the same candidate. View these two examples demonstrating the impact of manipulating digital media at PBS's Website: www.pbs.org/30secondcandidate/tricks_of_the_trade/

Digital Distribution

Ubiquitous distribution is a unique power of digital media. Each of us can now make a personal captivating digital story in a relatively short amount of time for a relatively small amount of money and share it quite literally with the whole world. The exchanging and sharing of these personal digital stories that can be shared with anyone, be they friend, foe or stranger, builds connections between people. Sharing our own stories and viewing the stories about others via the Internet, gives us the ability to cross our surrounding geographical and cultural boundaries, breaks down apathy, stereotypes and prejudices and enables us all to experience the humanity of our fellowman wherever they may live.

Once the stories have been completed, distribution is up to each storyteller. Unlike the book, television or the film industry, no publisher, film studio or other intermediary agent is needed to approve or distribute the finished piece.

The storyteller determines the final size and format as well as distribution channels for the digital story. What is useful depends on the purpose and intended audience. What is possible depends somewhat on type of hardware and software being used. It is quite inexpensive and easy to make multiple file formats for various distributions for friends, family, a circle of colleagues, local neighborhoods, business clients and as widely as world communities. Try one or enjoy them all.

In Conclusion

All storytelling is powerful. All stories communicate experiences to other human beings. They give us our history, heritage and sense of self. We need to ask what is unique about each medium, how users respond to it and how its potential can be realized. Whatever medium is used — oral telling, text stories, cinema, or digital media — good stories endure because storytellers artfully touch people's spirits and hearts.

Where a story comes from, whether it is familiar or a private memory, the retelling exemplifies the making of a connection.

~ Mary Catherine Bateson

Chapter 3

Storying Around Builds Useful 21st Century Skills

We are in the twilight of a society based on data. As information and intelligence become the domain of computers, society will place new value on the one human ability that can't be automated: emotion.

Imagination, myth, ritual, stories – the language of emotion – will affect everything from our purchasing decisions to how well we work and communicate with others.

~ Rolf Jensen, Dream Society

Information: The Raw Material of Change

We are witnesses of the most astounding changes ever experienced in a single human lifetime. Change has become relentless for all of us – in our communities, workplaces, schools, homes and personal lives. And hold on . . .our lives are expected to continue changing at an accelerating rate, largely because of the huge volume and availability of information.

Communication technologies particularly are a major driving force that increases the volume of information in our world. These technologies give us access and connections to endless data, people, and ideas across highly interactive media. It is believed that information doubles every 18 months. Over time it becomes difficult even to grasp how that alters our lives. More new information has been produced in the last 30 years than in the previous 5000. (Peter Large, *The Micro Revolution Revisited*) For example, 75% of what we know today didn't exist twenty years ago. And the sum total of what we have acquired today is still only considered 1% of what there is yet to know. (Tony Buzan, *Using Both Sides of Your Brain*) Consider that one issue of the NY Times has as much information in it as a person living in the Renaissance had to know in their lifetime. (Richard Wurman, *Information Anxiety*) Just think of the people who, in order to keep up their personal knowing, actually attempt to read the NY Times, the Wall Street Journal and their local paper in the same day. Whew!

This information explosion might more accurately be described as a constant barrage of data that is considered "raw material" influencing change exponentially. The faster information gets out into the world and into the minds of people, the faster people absorb it and combine and recombine it to create more new concepts, theories, facts and inventions. (DePorter, *Quantum Learning*) This situation generates increasing amounts of ideas, understandings and innovations that constantly define and redefine our way of living, learning, working and communicating.

We are creating and using up ideas and images at a faster and faster pace. Knowledge, like people, places, things and organizations, is becoming disposable.

~ Alvin Toffler, Future Shock

Before 1945

Consider the changes you or your parents have witnessed if you or they were born before 1945: At that time, you would never have heard of FM radios, tape recorders, electric typewriters, credit cards, ball-point pens, word processors, yogurt, dishwashers, clothes dryers, or air conditioning. There were no such things as laser beams, plastic, polio shots, frozen food, television, penicillin, pantyhose, personal computers, overseas calls, day-care centers, group therapy or nursing homes. For one nickel, you could ride a streetcar, make a phone call, buy a Pepsi or enough stamps to mail one letter and two postcards. You could buy a new Chevy Coupe if you had $600 but at least gas was being sold for 12 cents a gallon!

~ Anonymous

Preparing to Learn, Unlearn and Relearn

Communication technologies also contribute greatly to a newly globalized marketplace that puts increasingly competitive pressure on American products and jobs. Businesses and jobs that are viable today are not guaranteed to be there tomorrow. As jobs come and go, people are left with the challenge of making career transitions wisely and quickly. The skills and knowledge we learned for work can suddenly become obsolete overnight leaving us unwanted or unnecessary in the marketplace. We can no longer expect to have a single job for a lifetime. Students in schools today are expected to have up to twelve different careers. (Secretary Riley, 2000). *Learning a Living* is an apt title given to benchmark workplace studies conducted by the Secretary of Labor's Commission on Achieving Necessary Skills (SCANS). This commission focused on the kind of learning young people and workers already on the job need to nurture to be productive workers, responsible citizens and have what they need to live well. (http://wdr.doleta.gov/SCANS)

As we experience shifts in the job market, the skills needed to prosper also change. Everyone is going to need make an audacious commitment to learning to survive. It won't be enough to learn new things. We will need to be willing to also unlearn habits, beliefs, skills that have become obsolete or inhibiting to getting those next new jobs. The attitudes and skills for ongoing learning not only apply to future workers still in our schools but also to many adults who now face having more job changes than they ever expected when they graduated! The skills and competencies that served many past generations are not expected to continue to give people a prosperous living let alone prepare them to live full lives.

How do we stay valuable in a changing marketplace? What skills and competencies are needed to prosper? How do we prepare? How can we keep up? How do we unlearn? How do we learn to learn even after school is done? To answer these questions, the U.S. Department of Education has now defined 21st Century Skills. (www.21stcenturyskills.org) These skills encompass an urgent national agenda to build the minds and spirits of our citizenry so that we can prosper in these times of rapid change. Nationally, communities are making efforts to prepare children — as well as upgrade the skills of people already in the workforce — for 21st century living.

Children of the Ewe people of the Ghana are simply not considered educated unless they have heard many times the gliwo, animal stories that are intended to teach lessons in obedience, kindness, courage, honesty, and other virtues through indirect example.

~ Anne Pellowski, The World of Storytelling.

Storying Around and Around

It is easy to feel overwhelmed with the task of what we need to know and be able to do in this high tech era. Changing what we have always done or known creates confusion, uncertainty and anxiety. I don't believe that it is a coincidence that the growing personal digital storytelling trend has been emerging just at a time when we need to soothe our souls in these changing

21st Century Learning Skills

Here is an overview of four 21st century skill clusters identified by North Central Regional Lab (NCREL). For more details, visit www.ncrel.org/engauge/skills/21skills.htm.

Digital-Age Literacy

- Basic, Scientific, Economic, and Technical Literacies

- Visual and Information Literacies

- Multicultural Literacy and Global Awareness

Effective Communication

- Teaming, Collaboration, and Interpersonal Skills

- Personal, Social and Civic Responsibility

- Interactive Communication

Inventive Thinking

- Adaptability, Managing Complexity and Self-Direction

- Curiosity, Creativity, and Risk Taking

- Higher-Order Thinking and Sound Reasoning

High Productivity

- Prioritizing, Planning and Managing for Results

- Effective Use of Real-World Tools

- Ability to Produce Relevant, High Quality Products

times. Storytelling of all kinds anchors our spirits, our culture and our ability to make meaning of the chaotic world around us.

However, "storying around" by making lots of digital stories with digital media is not just playtime and heart-time for kids and adults – although there is nothing wrong with just having lots of fun and joy! Developing digital stories again and again will give us something even more. Creating stories provides us with important opportunities to build and practice a number of specific 21st skills as well as other types of learning people need in order to function in a knowledge society:

- Creativity and inventive thinking
- Multiple intelligences / learning styles
- Visual literacy
- Technical literacy
- Effective communication
- Evaluating effective communication
- Teaming and Collaboration
- Project management mentality
- Enduring understanding

Creativity and Inventive Thinking

Do you consider yourself creative? How inventive is your thinking? Where do good ideas come from? What emotions come up for you when you are asked to be creative or inventive for a project or problem? Many do not find joy in inventing something new or may feel incompetent when challenged with creative tasks. Others have an internal critic chanting to themselves and others, "I am NOT creative. I am NOT creative." Discouraging messages and experiences in our schools have left many disconnected from their natural creative talents.

This quantity over quality shift in our culture has created an even deeper need for truly informing experiences – for insight, the most precious form of information.

~ Nathan Sheddroff

Don't be too certain of learning the past from the lips of the present. Remember that what you are told is really threefold; shaped by the teller, reshaped by the listener; concealed from both by the dead man of the tale.

~ Valadimir Nabokof

From nothing something is formed. From imagination to conception and then into existence – that is creating!

~ Robert Fritz, Creativity.

Imagination is more important than knowledge

~ Albert Einstein

All art is technology

~ George Lucas

With the advent of Sputnik, the Russians launched the first space shuttle, opening a new era. Americans, in reaction to Sputnik, committed mass resources to improving math and science skills of all students in order to compete in the race to the moon. This political initiative re-directed national school curricula towards logic, mathematical, and science-based education. We made learning math and science an urgent national mission. However, we also allowed this math-science movement to inadvertently marginalize most of the art programs as being extra in school priorities. We also shifted our definition of what it meant to be an educated person. Funds and time for music, visual arts, dance, and theater are being challenged even more in today's political climate of standardized test scores.

However, Eric Jensen, author of *Arts with the Brain in Mind*, argues that the arts should be a major discipline. Not only do they help reach a range of learning styles but the arts also enhance the process of learning by developing a learner's integrated sensory, attentional, cognitive, emotional and motor capacities. Such brain systems are the driving forces behind all other learning connections, according to Jensen. They engage learners in making meaning out of data, give "sticky" power to ideas and concepts, and help learners integrate information between more than one subject area.

Digital storytelling uses both sides of the brain. Much is known about the brain today. Roger Sperry, a Nobel Prize Winner (1981), and Robert Ornstein are known worldwide for their work on brain waves and specialized functions. They identified two sides of the brain – left and right – each producing different types of mental activity. Subsequent researchers documented that encouraging people to develop both sides produced a synergetic effect increasing mental performance. We hold stereotypes of artists being right-brained and science-minded people being left-brained. However, great artists, scientists, inventors, and writers (Einstein, Picasso, Thomas Jefferson, and Leonardo da Vinci, for example) actually used their full range of brain capacity integrating both right and left sides simultaneously. Research has shown that it takes a synthesis of both left and right sides working back and forth between the corpus collosum's nerve fibers – it takes a whole brain to reach our creating and thinking potential. (www.viewzone.com/bicam.html.)

Creativity begins with imagination skills and strategies. Walt Disney built his empire with "Imagineering" strategies – inspiring people to dream the environments that eventually became the Disney Parks. Because the right side of the brain is random rather than sequenced like the left side, information stored there is available for combining and recombining into new patterns or thoughts. Generating ideas, concepts and new perspectives utilize right brain functions.

Brain Functions

While some of us generally favor one side of our brain functions over the other, the ultimate goal is to begin incorporating activities that enable us to practice strengthening our weaknesses. For fun, take an online brain style test and then plunge into activities that will build up your whole brain!

(http://faculty.indy.cc.ks.us/jnull/introtestrightbrain.htm)

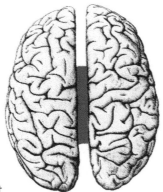

Left Brain

- language
- logic
- numbers
- sequence
- linearity
- analysis
- present and past

Right Brain

- rhythm
- music
- images
- imagination
- randomness
- color
- present and future

The more connection that can be made in the brain, the more integrated the experience is within memory.

~ Don Campbell

Everyone is creative, but some people don't let new ideas surface. If you want to be creative, you have to be able to suppress your internal critics for just one minute.

~ Marvin Minsky, Society of Mind.

An often missed step of problem-solving is the ability to generate creative solutions to consider. Once ideas are developed, the left brain's analysis function helps to sort out what to keep. But our creativeness needs time and permission to invent good, wild and out-of-the-box thoughts before being judged. It is difficult to develop critical thinking skills needed for decision making if you have little or nothing to consider.

Angeles Arrien, a cultural anthropologist, tells a story in her Wisdom Tales workshop about a meeting in Washington D.C. that brought together leaders from the across the nation to work on an environmental issue. Most of the leaders who spoke simply outlined the problems from their points of view. Finally a Navajo elder came forward to take his turn. He had been chosen to speak for all the people on the reservations. The Navajo elder started his speaking turn with gratitude for being invited to be part of these conversations, then he spoke of what was working and what should be kept. He then shared what was not working. But he ended by saying, "I regret that I only have three creative solutions to offer to this situation. I am below the indigenous standard of being expected to bring at least 10 creative solutions to the circle!"

Another story that Angeles Arrien shared concerned the storytelling skills of the African Dogon tribe. Every evening, the tribal members gather at their fires. Starting at the early age of five, everyone is expected to take a turn telling stories. Each Dogon tribal member expects to practice telling both actual stories and invented stories without revealing to their listeners the difference. Listeners are expected to practiced discerning the difference by commenting on what about the shared story made it seem real or imagined. While many Americans would devalue these invented stories as not real, labeling them fake or lies, the Dogon members are actually mastering an important aspect of problem-solving skills. They were learning to spontaneously invent situations or scenarios with enough details so real as to be believed true and possible. Today this same skill is employed to generate imagined future visions. Creating imagined stories is an art form among the Dogon that has gained their tribe a regional reputation. From far and wide, the Dogon tribe members are invited to help mediate and problem-solve difficult situations. Their highly developed skills of creativity and invented thinking have become an incredible foundation for imagining believable solutions to problems and situations.

One of the most effective ways of opening people to creativity is through digital stories. Adults who might never have had these creative experiences in schools, as well as students who still have little exposure, can now discover their personal uniqueness along with increased artistic and academic talents. By the end of their experience in **DigiTales Storytelling Camps**, participants now know and tell a different story about their own creative abilities.

So come and tell a digital story – become creative in designing and communicating with the images, graphics, movement and music of digital media. Mix and dance them together until you bring into form something that did not exist before — something that only exists because of your creativity, imagination and willingness to tell a story that needs to be told. Who knows what other experiences will open up for you as your natural creative self is nourished and gains practice and experience!

Being creative organizes existing elements into new and different wholes to produce desired results - combining and recombining.

~ Hanks and Perry, Wake up Your Creative Genius

Imagination...

Imagination has brought mankind through the dark ages to its present state of civilization. Imagination has given us the steam engine, the telephone, the talking-machine, and the automobile; for these things had to be dreamed of before they became realities. So I believe that dreams — daydreams, you know, with your eyes wide open and your brain machinery whizzing — are likely to lead to the betterment of the world. The imaginative child will become the imaginative man or woman most apt to invent, and therefore to foster, civilization.

~ L. Frank Baum

Multiple Intelligences and Learning Styles

Do you consider yourself smart? What is your intelligence quotient (IQ)? What emotions come up for you when you take on something new that reveals what you know and what you don't know? Not all of us left school feeling gifted because the place called school values a very limited definition of intelligence. The curriculum, learning activities and assessments in schools today incorporate very few learning styles to measure success. This practice leaves many believing that they are not smart as defined by their school experiences regardless of their success in the world.

Howard Gardner, a Harvard psychologist, built a framework for multiple intelligences upon right-left brain research. He broadly defines intelligence as "the capacity to solve problems or to fashion products that are valued in one or more cultures." His work expanded the early right-left brain research that - while still credible — was later found to be too simplistic. The brain is more complex than early discoveries had documented. Gardner's research and studies have identified at least eight different kinds of intelligence located in different parts of the brain: logical-mathematical, musical-rhythmic, bodily-kinesthetic, verbal-linguistic, visual-spatial, naturalistic, interpersonal and intrapersonal.

Our society values only two or three of the eight types of intelligence when deciding who's smart and who's not. (Howard Gardner, *Frames of Mind*). Other cultures put a different emphasis on these intelligences. Thomas Armstrong, author of *In Their Own Way*, gives cultural examples like the Anang society of Nigeria, who develop musical and bodily-kinesthetic intelligences. They are able to sing hundreds of songs, play numerous instruments, and execute complex dances. In Eskimo cultures, Armstrong points out that spatial intelligence is a major strength. Each of these cultures defines "smart" in a different way.

> The part of the brain that thrives on worksheets and teacher lectures probably takes up less that 1 percent of the total (brain) available for learning.
>
> ~ Thomas Armstrong, In Their Own Way

Today's schools are still organized primarily around verbal-linguistic and logical-mathematical abilities. These are the same areas focused on after the Sputnik event. If you are naturally talented in either of these two out of eight intelligences you will be honored in school and assumed to be ready for success in life. School and even some business intelligence tests measure these same two abilities. And today's accountability tests, which are being mandated for all students, use the sole intelligence of verbal-linguistics to conduct the actual assessment. Even after many studies and much research, these statewide tests still continue to focus on only these two intelligences. When educators have found ways to honor and integrate diverse thinking and learning styles, more learners find success.

Creating digital stories opens up opportunities to experience, nurture and practice a range of intelligences. Kids and adults who have natural abilities in music, visual, spatial or kinesthetic intelligences find working with digital media allows them to tap into their innate strengths. Digital media gives learners more options for taking in information, making sense of ideas, and expressing thinking and understanding. They can now express their smartness and have additional ways of demonstrating their learning and thinking. They also have visible talents to share with others, as evidenced by their skill with digital media.

Digital storytelling accesses both sides of the brain. The challenge of using digital media to express ideas provides opportunities for all of us to be multi-minded by practicing a range of intelligences. Brainstorming that uses a mind mapping process accesses the imagination function of the right brain. Writing the script makes use of the verbal-linguistic side of the left-brain. Storyboarding uses the logical-mathematical side of the brain. Using images, music, and color makes use of the functions of the right side of the brain. Scanning photos, keyboarding, and working with cameras engages the bodily kinesthetic intelligence. Integrating these media elements together accesses both sides of the brain. Here's to enjoying all your creative and critical functions as you make a story!

Much traditional teaching is based on the model of a pipeline through which knowledge passes from teacher to students. The role of a teacher (today) is to create the conditions for invention rather than provide ready-made knowledge.

~ Seymour Papert

Again, we all need lots of experiences that integrate both sides of the brain in order to increase fluency with a range of intelligences. Learning disabilities occur when we are limited in the ways we are able to learn, create meanings and communicate our understandings. Many of the messages in this book give suggestions but then direct you to do it your way! Being able to use all parts of our brain, accessing a variety of intelligences and using a multitude of learning styles lets us bring more talent and flexibility to our lives and work places. Using both parts of the brain increases our thinking and creating in all areas of our lives. We can have fun making digital stories and the processes we use to do so give our brains a work out at the same time.

Visual Literacy

Do you consider yourself an educated media consumer? How effective are you in using images to communicate? Do you use visuals to "decorate " or supplement your written work? Or do you use text and words to supplement your visual messages? How would you rate your skills in reading, interpreting, making meaning or creating images? What emotions come up for you when you are asked to draw, paint, photograph, or create video images to express or communicate ideas and thoughts?

Our personal and professional world is inundated with images from television, movies, presentations, and magazines. What would the world of marketing, publishing, advertising or politics be without the use of images to persuade and influence? Visual literacy has become an essential communication skill. While verbal literacy involves a person's ability to interpret and use spoken and written language – to decode the world of words – visual literacy relates to a person's ability to interpret and create visual information, to understand images of all kinds and use them to communicate more effectively. (Lynell Burmark, *Visual Literacy: Learn to See, See to Learn.*)

Visual literacy contributes to developing visual-spatial intelligence – one of the eight intelligences identified by Howard Gardner. It has become an essential literacy we urgently need in today's world of data overload, in which we are required to absorb and manage mass quantities of information. Research by 3M Corporation shows that people can process visual information 60,000 times more quickly than textual information. (3M's, *Polishing Your Presentations*) Richard Lindstrom, author of *The Business Week Guide to Multimedia Presentations*, explains that the eyes are the most powerful information conduits to the brain. He reveals that information that is sent to the

Dear God, I didn't think purple and orange went together until I saw the sunset you created on Tuesday. That was cool.

~ Eugene. Shared by Lynell Burmark in her book, Visual Literacy

How do I know what I think until I see what I say?

~ E. M. Forster

Reading in the pure literary sense was mugged on its way to the 21st century by the electronic media, which influenced and changed how we read. Printed text lost its monopoly to another communication technology, film. Film makes the time-consuming burden of learning to decode and digest words seem obsolete.

~ Will Eisner, Graphic Storytelling and Visual Narrative

brain processes through two optic nerves consisting of 1,000,000 nerve fibers. Auditory nerves only have 30,000 fibers each. Nerve cells devoted to visual processing account for approximately 30% of the brain's cortex, compared to 8% for touch and 3% for hearing. With all that visual bandwidth, it is no wonder we can be more efficient in learning and communicating using visual language.

Visual literacy is also one of the key 21st Century skills identified by the U.S. Department of Education in order for citizens to prosper in work and life. Visual literacy is not just about seeing – which we all certainly do. Passively watching television does not mean our brains are necessarily engaged. Seeing an image does not automatically ensure learning from it. Decoding visual stimuli and learning from visual images requires practice. Imagery can shift attitudes and opinions through visual and emotional impact, attitudes that are often less susceptible to change through print. Print relies upon the readers' ability to interpret abstract symbols; visuals are more direct and emotional. (Dr. Mary Alice White, *The Third Learning Revolution*) Visually literate people will need to consciously read and write with images to become knowing consumers and creators of media information.

Communication is more effective using visuals. Comprehension and retention are increased through visuals. A 1966 study sponsored by 3M at University of Minnesota School of Management found that visual aids are 43% more effective in persuading audience members to take action than presentations without visuals. Presenters using visuals were also rated higher than those presenters with no visuals.

Digital storytelling by its very nature requires us to learn and practice visual literacy skills. Working with digital media is a perfect way to experiment and experience using a visual language. Authors begin to learn effective uses of media attributes like color, style, shape, size, pacing and movement along with careful selection of appropriate and effective images to communicate their meanings. The images chosen for a story become symbolic, emotive, and engaging in such a way that if they were not there, it would be less of a story or have less impact for the viewer. We can experiment with finding an artful visual expression of ideas and thoughts. A great deal of analysis is required to pick and choose how to design a story's visual elements. What experiences do you want to create for your viewer? How will your choices develop that experience? What meanings are conveyed and understood by others? Finally, personal and peer reflections on the final product can offer feedback on the effectiveness of your communication through images. Take note of what worked and what you would do differently next time.

Using images also helps authors economize their stories by showing ideas, feelings, and information rather than telling the story with words. Keep your eye out for images that extend the story and are not simply used as decoration for the voiceover. Are you providing literal images that match the text? If you are talking about a tree, do we see a tree being shown? If you are talking about a horse, do we see a horse being shown? Or can you select images that will provide non-verbal symbolic meanings, information or feelings that viewers wouldn't experience in the story without them. Visuals that extend the story become an essential part of the tale. Making digital stories gives us a forum for

Young people learn more than half of what they know from visual information.

~ Mary Alice White, researcher, Columbia Teacher's College.

In a society where powerful interests employ visual data to persuade (info-tactics) — schools must show students how to look beyond the surface to understand deeper levels of meaning and the tactics employed to sway their thinking.

~ Alvin Toffler, Future Shock.

learning the visual grammar and vocabulary needed to both understand and present concepts and ideas using images.

Technical Literacy

How do you rate your technology skills? What hardware and software skills do you have? What skills do you wish you had if you had the time and dime to learn? What emotions come up for you when you are asked to use technologies you don't know yet? Technology literacy is more than knowing equipment and software tools, although there are plenty of skills to learn. Technical literacy is about using these tools in powerful and creative ways that increase thinking, problem-solving and communicating.

Technology is a term that applies to any equipment or software that extends our ability to learn, think and produce. It is impossible to predict the next technical tools that will be essential for learning and working in the future. But we do know that having technical skills is a major factor in determining wages today and will continue to become more important in the future. Some studies estimate that, on average, IT jobs pay 85% more than other jobs (Pociask, 2002). The U.S. Department of Commerce also reports that "workers who use a computer at work can earn 17 to 22% more than other workers." Even in non-IT industries, most analysts agree that technologically skilled workers are likely to earn higher wages than those without such skills. (Economics and Statistics Administration, 2002)

The International Society of Technology Education (ISTE) is an international organization that has outlined a highly adopted set of technology standards for students, teachers and administrators called National Education Technology Standards (NETS.) Schools are working diligently to ensure that all students have these essential technical skills. There are a myriad of issues including a growing digital divide that identifies specific groups that are not getting access and experiences with technology, including females, minorities and low economic groups. Hopefully a national agenda that encourages tech-

It [the computer] is the first metamedium, and as such it has degrees of freedom for representation and expression never before encountered and as yet barely investigated.

~ Alan Kay

nological literacy for all will succeed in addressing these issues and provide us with a new generation of graduates who will be fluent with technical skills. (www.iste.org/standards).

Meanwhile, there are a lot of adults who left school before technology was part of the curriculum. They are searching for ways to catch up with these techno-savvy kids. Lots of jokes are made about adults who are unable to program their VCRs without turning to someone under the age of ten. Technical skills do not seem to come as naturally to adults as to kids. Teachers in particular are expected to develop and assess lessons using technology when they have never done their own multimedia communication projects. This idea can be compared to asking someone to coach basketball who has never played the game. You make a better coach for kids if you know the game from the inside out. Teachers are dealing with the difficult job of acquiring their own technical skills while being expected to teach students what they hardly know themselves.

One delightful way to engage teachers as well as parents, senior citizens, business people and many others in learning these technologies is through a digital storytelling camp. DigiTales Storytelling Camps provide an experiential hands-on three days of working together and learning whatever technical skills are needed to create something very personal. This personal immersion invites people to have fun and enjoy learning while working on a story project that means something to them. Good positive learning environments nurture personal interests, enabling learners to get past the anxiety or difficulties of learning something new. The fun and passion of creating a personal story provides the context for learning hardware and software tools. Making your own personal movie generates a kind of magical enthusiasm that drives participants to learn what they need to know about technology tools. They remember the skills because they expect to continue using them to make more digital stories. This is significantly different than taking a class to learn a software package from beginning to end. While there are multiple pieces of hardware and software packages involved in digital storytelling, functions are learned as ameans to getting your story told.

Ours is the age which is proud of machines that think and suspicious of men who try to.

~ Howard Mumford Jones

If technology works, it is obsolete.

~ Marshall MuLuhan

ISTE National Education Technology Standards for Students (NETS•S)

Many of the following skills and understandings can be obtained through digital storytelling activities. (www.iste.org/standards)

Basic Operations and Concepts

- Students demonstrate a sound understanding of the nature and operation of technology systems
- Students are proficient in the use of technology

Social, Ethical, and Human Issues

- Students understand the ethical, cultural, and societal issues related to technology
- Students practice responsible use of technology
- Students develop positive attitudes toward technology uses

Technology Productivity Tools

- Students use technology to enhance learning
- Students use technology tools to collaborate in constructing technology-enhanced models, prepare publications, and produce other creative works.

Technology Communication Tools

- Students use telecommunications to collaborate, publish, and interact with peers, experts, and other audiences
- Students use a variety of media and formats to communicate information and ideas effectively to multiple audiences.

Technology Research Tools

- Students use technology to locate, evaluate, and collect information from a variety of sources
- Students use technology tools to process data and report results

Technology Problem-Solving and Decision-making Tools

- Students use technology resources for solving problems and making decisions
- Students employ technology in the development of strategies for solving problems in the real world.

Identifying Standards for Digital Storytelling

Nationally, standards guide our student's curriculum and course-work. These standards are the outcomes of what we want all students to know and understand in any project or unit. Teachers wanting to organize digital storytelling worry that this time will take away from meeting the accountability demands issued through No Child Left Behind (NCLB). Kentucky's Scott County School District teachers were involved in a yearlong exploration of shifting the writing process from paper to the silver screen. The focus on accountability was dragging enthusiasm for writing down until they experienced creating personal narrative stories. Digital storytelling is concerned with writing skills and communicating in the 21st Century. The following standards were identified for Scott County's Digital Storytelling.

(www.ncrel.org/engauge/resource/stories/scott.htm)

(www.scott.k12.ky.us/technology/digitalstorytelling)

Primary Content Area Addressed: Writing
21st Century Skill Cluster Addressed: Effective Communication
Primary Skills

- Interactive Communication
- Interpersonal Skills
- Personal and Social Responsibility
- Technological Literacy

Secondary Skills

- Relevant, High-Quality Products
- Basic Literacy
- Visual Literacy
- Curiosity, Creativity, and Risk-Taking

Effective Communication

Do you believe you have something important to say? How would you rank your ability to communicate ideas and thinking to others? What emotions come up for you when you are asked to write, speak, make a movie or create other information products? As we imagine ideas, make meaning of data factoids, or discover new concepts, it is essential to be able to communicate these thoughts effectively to others.

Imagine that important science work like that performed by Einstein or Edison was forever lost to us because they could not or did not communicate their ideas and discoveries. Or consider our losses if other inventors, leaders, religious thinkers, cultural anthropologists, or businessmen who lived and learned never communicated their experiences to us. Ironically, Socrates (469-399), who still lives on in the history of influential ideas, wrote nothing because he felt that knowledge was a living, interactive thing. He was appalled and opposed to using written words and gave many warnings that words would diminish the intellectual development of man. Most of our knowledge of Socrates' work and ideas comes from Plato's writings. It is Plato's account of Socrates' life that outlines one of Socrates' most famous philosophical ideas: the necessity of doing what one thinks is right even in the face of universal opposition. And the art of using Socratic dialogue (inquiry) still influences great thinkers and learners today thanks to Plato being an effective communicator with the new technology of his day – words.

Effective communication starts with having great content that is worth sharing. As you determine how to package your thoughts, knowing your purpose and your audience begins to shape the content, approach and medium of the message you want to communicate. Delivery modes have definitely expanded with each new technology. We have many more new and varied choices than Socrates ever imagined, but the goal of thinking and communicating has changed very little. Media available for telling our stories include oral, handwritten, printed, play scripts, television scripts, film, multimedia movies and

Children are native to cyberspace and we, as adults, are immigrants.

~ Douglas Rushkoff, Playing the Future

Today, if you are not confused, you are just not thinking clearly.

~ U. Peter

presentations, DVD, and the World Wide Web (WWW) incorporating many media. The challenge is to appreciate each medium and strive to create effective communication with whichever one(s) you use.

Digital storytelling involves mastering a variety of digital media. Putting together still photos, animations, video, music, sounds, titles, transitions, and other special effects challenges an author to understand the use of each element, and then decide how to make them work together effectively. But ah-h-h, the joy of your first completed piece! Creating digital stories gives everyone a unique experience of discovering their talent and originality. They now know they have something worth sharing with others. With each piece of work, they learn a little more about effective communication.

Effective Digital Communication

What do you look for in effective digital products? What criteria do you use to determine quality? What emotions come up for you when you are asked to communicate your ideas, concepts and thinking with digital media rather than speaking or writing? Few people claim to be competent with oral or written communication let alone digital media. And after mastering the media's functions, you will find utter personal pleasure in using digital media to make your ideas, concepts and thinking come alive!

The medium is the message according to Marshall McLuhan. Each medium used influences in its own way how we represent our information. With each medium you are designing information – shaping it and forming it into a communication piece that will reach out to others. These varied medias require unique skills and competencies in order to master both technical and artful uses. Just because we can speak does not mean we are powerful at oration. Many speech classes and coaches are dedicated to helping people excel at this medium. The same is true of writing, using cameras, desktop publishing, video and using multimedia. Just knowing the medium itself doesn't ensure that it will be used in creative, effective ways.

Quintilian (ca. 35-96 A.C.E.) wrote that there were three styles of communication: low, or plain, style was best suited for instruction; the middle style for moving an audience; and the high style for charming the audience.

Digital media is a great multidimensional communication tool (multimedia) because it combines images, text, sound and animation, and creates all sorts of sensory experiences to engage viewers. However, like other media before it, learning the mechanics of the tools does not necessarily mean you are able to create effective communications. It is even possible that by overemphasizing the technology, the message may miss its mark. Many of today's digital information products are more sizzle than content. Users become distracted by the bells and whistles and are not necessarily guided to deepen their understanding of the tool or what it can offer in terms of effective communication.

With the deluge of information in all our lives, a key factor for effective communication is to consider what makes your piece stand out or be memorable. Does it engage and move your viewers in some way? Do viewers really understand your experience, message, concept, or idea? How effective was your craftsmanship in using multimedia technologies to shape and form the story? Craftsmanship encompasses the design of the information in your communication piece. What is the tone, emotion and content provided by the text fonts, color, and size along with images, voice, sound, or music used, along with the overall design and presentation of the content?

Effective communication with both content and craftsmanship is directly related to how the information piece is received by listeners. Most digital stories need to meet only the criteria set by the storyteller, since the audience and purpose are strictly personal. Other digital stories are developed to share with a wider audience. Whether your digital story is personal or meant for a specific audience, one simple informal measure of success is the reaction of listeners. Good, effective communication pieces engender strong emotional reactions like crying, laughing, disagreement, amusement, dislike or delight. The kiss of death is indifference from viewers.

A set of formal design guidelines that can more directly coach digital storytellers to increase their effectiveness with digital media have been created. These comprehensive scoring guides encourage looking at how the craftsmanship of using the technical elements impacts of the communication of the con-

The medium is the message.

~ Marshall McLuhan

The digital revolution is far more significant than the invention of writing or even of printing.

~ Douglas Engelbart, Inventor of the Computer Mouse.

Digital Media Scoring Guides

The online Digital Media Scoring Guides consist of two parts: Part I: Content Communication and Part II: Craftsmanship of Communication. Each of the two parts carries equal weight in creating effective communications. The traits used in Content Communication were constructed using national benchmarks for genres of writing that will differ depending upon the type of communication being created. The traits used in Craftsmanship of Communication were developed and prototyped to represent the function of technologies. For more detailed descriptions of the nine traits, resources, and training materials in effectively using these online scoring guides, Bernajean's *Evaluating Digital Products* book is available online as well. (www.digitales.us)

Part I: Content Communication

- Preparation Process
- Content Knowledge
- Format / Organization

Part II: Craftsmanship of Communication

- Text Communication
- Image Communication
- Voice / Sound Communication
- Design of Communication
- Presentation Communication
- Interactivity of Communication

tent. These guidelines have been combined into a tool called Digital Media Scoring Guides (p.67). While these scoring guides were originally developed, prototyped and validated to help teachers raise the quality of student digital products, they are also useful for anyone ready to design effective products. An online version of the Digital Media Scoring Guides is available for personal use at the www.digitales.us Website under "Evaluating Projects." Bernajean's book, *Evaluating Digital Products*, is a resource for reflecting on the quality of digital media products.

Teaming and Collaboration

There are great benefits to working together! Collaboration skills are useful to both children and adults. Through collaboration, teams share the work of ambitious projects, exchange diverse ideas, and generally increase productivity along with the quality of their work.

Snowflakes are one of nature's most fragile things, but just look at what they can do when they stick together.

~ Vesta Kelly

Filmmaking particularly lends itself to large groups dividing up all the tasks with the director coordinating the process. Nikkos Theodosakis is a film artist who outlines and inspires these skills and processes with filmmaking in his book, *The Director in the Classroom*. Nikkos defines filmmaking as a collaborative art, requiring dozens of passionate craftspeople to bring a focused vision onto the screen.

However, the digital storytelling approach used in this book is a very personal one that focuses on making and sharing the meaning you make of experiences with information, learning, family, events and decisive moments in your life. It is a first person story shared from the heart rather than the head. There is not a team of task specialists who capture your story and edit it into a final product. You choose the story you want to tell. You write the script and put it together using photos, captions, simple animation, video, voice over and music.

The collaboration found in this digital storytelling approach is in the process of making digital stories together rather than jointly contributing to creating a common product. Storytellers depend upon each other to help develop their own individual stories and to use the technologies. The group supports each other through coaching, teaching, reflecting, cheerleading, and celebrating. This group approach to creating digital stories has a very profound impact of developing personal pride as well as building team and community spirits.

If more than one person is creating a single story, then it is essential that the script be co-developed and reflective of each person's experiences and thinking. While the task of gathering and preparing resources can be shared as well as production tasks, the group digital story still needs to retain a personal approach rather than moving into a third person perspective of telling and observing events. Their collaborative digital product should not look like a stitched quilt of each doing a portion and then rotating in each individual's segments. Working together makes the storyboard have a serious role in creating a coherent flowing digital story giving the group an agreed upon road map for all of them to follow.

Project Management Mentality

How well are you able to execute long-term projects containing multiple steps and process stages? How competent do you feel to plan and monitor the progress of large-scale projects? What emotions are charged for you in managing your time, deadlines, and problem-solving barriers?

While reading Melvin Levine's *The Myth of Laziness*, I realized that digital storytelling was an experience that represented one of his points of valuing the development of a project mentality. The ideas discussed in this section are gleaned directly from Levine's work but also emerge from my own experiences of teaching adults and kids.

When computers or people are networked together, their power multiplies geometrically.

~ Scott McNeely

Light is the task where many share the toil.

~ Homer

One of the greatest labor saving inventions of today is tomorrow.

~ Vincent T. Ross

Levine talks a great deal about "output" failure that creates a real hardship for adults in the workplace and also plagues our students' success in classrooms. Through most of our schooling, assignments and tasks are chunked down into manageable work pieces, especially where they concern developing communication products. Among the many skills Levine believes that need to be coached and practiced directly in school is the experience of long-term projects that are organized and developed over extended periods of time. These involve multiple steps or stages needed to reach the project goal(s) and deadlines. The work itself is perfected by "sanding and polishing" the ideas and thinking until they represent the best of what can be at that time. This practice shapes habits and attitudes that can be used over and over in the perfection of any worthy, long-term venture, from rebuilding an antique automobile to compiling a grant to executing a business plan.

Levine suggests that it is not just about having larger projects or doing the work over longer time frames. Key to the enterprise is an attitude of workmanship towards the project – doing whatever it takes to ensure quality and effectiveness. Writing, for example, is often assigned in time-crunch situations for students, creating the experience of performing a "brain sprint." This fosters an attitude of getting it done – known as "get in and get out" work habits. Whereas a marathon-type approach occurs in the form of a "project" that is worked out, worked over and reworked into a polished example of craftsmanship.   The marathon-type approach offers students much more by helping to develop a project management mentality, which will serve them well throughout their lives. (Melvin Levine, *The Myth of Laziness*)

Digital storytelling includes multiple process steps that develop a range of project mentality skills. Making a digital story that others will likely view has stressful learning curves, challenging problems to solve to get your ideas into form, pacing the work, managing the deadlines and continuous reflection on how the work is evolving. But the struggles are what provide the personal rewards – you take the creative challenge knowing that even though you may encounter challenges, giving birth to your own digital story is a worthwhile

Project Management Mentality Skills

A number of "soft" process skills considered project management mentality skills are practiced in any digital storytelling project.

- Defining the project goal or outcome
- Planning the scope and steps needed to reach the goal
- Identifying and gathering together people, information, and resources
- Organizing resources and time
- Time management for pacing and meeting deadlines
- Learning whatever is needed to accomplish the goal
- Problem-solving barriers
- Collaborating as needed
- Reflecting on content and process
- Revising, polishing, reworking towards quality
- Sustaining fortitude through the complexity and multiple stages until completion
- Meeting deadlines

experience. Every digital story's public showing brings an exhilarating experience which is one of the great side effects when investments made by the storytellers yields something that was worth doing. What they learned along the way is evident in the finished product and is appreciated by all.

Enduring Understanding

Everyone in the 21st century needs to consider themselves learners. Helping people of all ages be better learners is big and important business today. Ongoing learning means never really being out of school. As you learn all the new skills associated with digital storytelling, notice all the ways you add to your own field of understanding.

One of the growing practices pushing against the boredom of drill and practice curriculum in schools that are overly focused on standardized tests is a movement called project-based learning. This approach to learning engages students in deeper thinking and engages deeper experiences with key concepts in order to develop their expertise in a variety of areas. The goal of project-based learning is that students develop enduring understanding of ideas and concepts rather than simply having short-term memory of facts for their one-time tests. Students engage in authentic work guided by critical questions. The expertise developed by students during their inquiry and problem-solving projects is translated into information products that are useful and beneficial to others. This approach is frequently called "constructivism" – students learn to construct their own meaning of information rather than feeding back what they are told they should know. Technology tools used for research and communication are very powerful mind tools when the learning quest drives their use. It takes time to engage students in project-based learning but what students learn has more "sticking" or long-term memory power.

Using digital stories to make meaning of what has been learned uses the power of stories and multimedia to convey information. Even though developing fictional stories definitely has its own value, the power of digital storytelling that is used for reflecting and relating real events is especially important for learning. (See Stories as Understandings discussed in *Chapter 1: That Reminds Me of a Story That Needs to Be Told*.) Instructional Technology (IT) when used to construct personal digital stories enables students to move from working with data factoids to enduring understanding of concepts.

Thread the beads of your facts together with a (story) plot so they don't roll away.

~ Annette Simons, The Story Factor

I forget what I was taught. I only remember what I have learnt.

~ Patrick White

Research on The Impact of Media and Technology in Schools

A very interesting research study describes the results of two groups of eighth graders studying the American Civil War. One group, called the control group, was instructed via traditional classroom practices of lectures, readings, and testing for facts. The other group, called the design group, worked on constructing multimedia projects. Students had to conceptualize, design, and construct their own projects. Both groups were given tests on their knowledge with no significant differences found. But the surprise occurred when a year later, researchers found that students in the control group remembered almost nothing about the historic content. But in contrast, the students in the design group were able to elaborate on concepts and ideas that extended beyond the historic facts. This is called enduring understandings. Technology played a significant part in learning, constructing and then communicating their ideas. The full research document can be reviewed at www.athensacademy.org/instruct/media_tech/reeves0.html.

It is possible to store the mind with a million facts and still be entirely uneducated.

~ Alex Bourne

In Conclusion

DigiTales Storytelling Camps are fun, meaningful and worth doing just for the sheer pleasure of doing it. Ask anyone who has already dared venture the adventure. But if that is not enough, it turns out digital storytelling is also good for the brain along with developing a number of 21st Century skills. If you find yourself ready to take the plunge, find or create your own digital storytelling camp. This book is meant to help you with ideas and resources to go for it!

Short-term memory skills do not an educated person make.

~ Richard Wurman

The whole fabric of honeybee society depends on communication ~ on an innate ability to send and receive messages, to encode and decode information.

~ The Honey Bee

For parents, teachers and other adults who missed these skills in their own school life, it is even more important to get involved in the struggles and experiences of making your own personal narrative digital stories. **DigiTales Storytelling Camps** demystify technology and increase practical fun uses of the technical tools for inexperienced adults. After experiencing the success of making your own digital stories, you are now ready to join or even lead others in becoming even more effective communicators with the technologies of our era – digital media.

Chapter 4

Conjuring Up Story Ideas

Enhanced through digital media and shared via the Web, digital stories become a powerful tool for improving your business, your creative vision, your community, and your bottom line.

~ Dana and Denise Atchley

Life is Full of Stories

This chapter is not for those who already have a head full of story ideas and uses for digital storytelling. Conjuring up story ideas are for those with the misconception that they cannot be storytellers or may not presently have a multitude of uses for stories. When asked to find a story, some experience a blank screen blocking their creative part that is really just waiting in the wings to express itself. Whether you think of yourself as a storyteller or not, you have since childhood shared stories about yourself, your beliefs and your understanding of the world around you. Life is quite simply full of stories! Now is a fun and perfect time to claim your own story!

Telling your story in first person is the hallmark of an exemplar digital story. Regardless of which type of story you decide to conjure up, remember that at the heart of all stories is the importance of expressing your own story. Make sure the story you tell develops your own thinking, spirit and viewpoint regardless of the content. Be very present in all your stories. A story is made especially powerful by "performing" it with your voice in personal mode rather than observer in "reading" mode. The power is not in telling about an event or someone else's life but rather shifting the lens to using the settings, details and actions as the context for telling YOUR own story with the experience. Each story needs to develop a very personal point, a moral, an a-ha awareness or a specific understanding. How does the historical or current event affect your life or thinking or beliefs? How has your family's history given meaning to or shaped your life? How does knowing the facts about a famous person or event influence your thinking and beliefs? Trust your own voice and unique approach to tell your stories. The magic is that if a story touches you — then that is the story that needs to be told!

Writing is easy. All you do is sit staring at a blank sheet of paper until the drops of blood form on your forehead.

~ Gene Fowler

Sometimes a person needs a story more than they need food to stay alive.

~ Barry Lopez

The following nine digital storytelling categories provide a range of ideas and uses for digital storytelling. Useful websites are also cited to network you with others exploring these uses. Examples of these types of digital stories when copyright-available are posted at www.digitales.us.

- Personal Stories: Creating Living Memories
- Kinship Stories: Family Stories of Who We Are
- Hyper-Interactive Stories: Group Stories with Diverse Paths and Endings
- Personal Expression: Creating Visual Expressions of Thoughts and Feelings
- Myths, Legends and Tales: Past, Present and Future
- Informative or Expository Stories: Information Beyond Words
- Persuasive Stories: Influencing and Impacting Others
- Itza Wrap: Stories of Lessons Learned
- Future Vision Stories: Imagining the Future NOW

A Personal Story Prompt

In our lives, there are moments, decisive moments, when the direction of our lives was shaped or reshaped. A major achievement, the time of a particularly bad setback, a decision made or not made, meeting a special person, the end of a relationship, the death of a loved one, or an unexpected challenging event are all examples of these fork-in-the-road decisive experiences. Right now, at this second, write about a decisive moment in your life on a 4 X 6 note card. Take 10 minutes. Adapted from Joe Lambert, author of Digital Storytelling.

Personal Stories: Creating Living Memories

These stories are personal experiences. Even as a child your life immediately began to fill up with stories of you. As a young or aging adult your string of accumulated stories now defines who you are, what you believe and how you choose to live your life. The stories that we tell ourselves and others reveal who we think we are along with identifying our purpose, meaning, and worth in life. Telling personal stories publicly celebrates our life.

Increasingly, I realized that I could not merely tell his story. Rather, I would have to tell MY story about him.

~ Ronald Steel

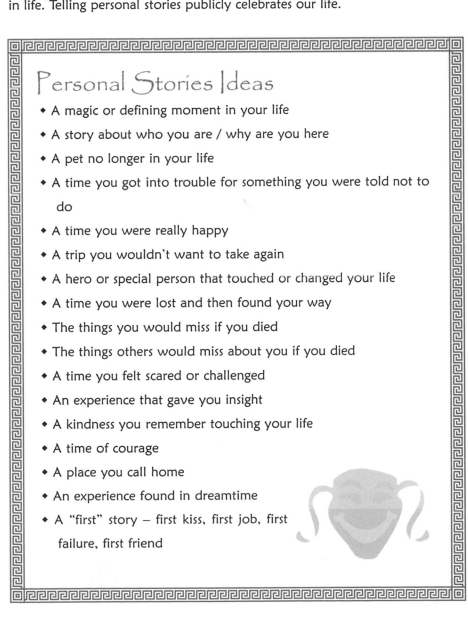

Personal Stories Ideas

- A magic or defining moment in your life
- A story about who you are / why are you here
- A pet no longer in your life
- A time you got into trouble for something you were told not to do
- A time you were really happy
- A trip you wouldn't want to take again
- A hero or special person that touched or changed your life
- A time you were lost and then found your way
- The things you would miss if you died
- The things others would miss about you if you died
- A time you felt scared or challenged
- An experience that gave you insight
- A kindness you remember touching your life
- A time of courage
- A place you call home
- An experience found in dreamtime
- A "first" story – first kiss, first job, first failure, first friend

A Living Memories Story Script: Da Um Jeitinho

Having a horse wasn't just about me having a pet. I really was in dire need of some safer way to round up our fifty milking cows up from their pasture . . . every morning AND . . . every night. I had had it stepping in gooey cow piles or getting stickers in my feet, let alone the terror of trying to stay out of the way of that nasty bull who snorted and charged at me whenever he saw me invading his private harem.

"No, You can't have a horse." I couldn't believe this was dad's response to my very practiced pitiful plea to finally have my own horse. At age seven, I was clear in my mind that a horse was exactly what I still needed and wanted. I heard Dad say "no" but it was definitely the wrong answer.

Well, if cows were creating my dilemma . . . then cows would be part of my solution. I became determined to train one of our new cows to be my horse. I didn't imagine it being hard . . . I saw it happening perfectly in my mind. I chose the cow, borrowed my grandpa's horse blankets and harnesses stored in the back of the shed, and vowed to have a horse of my own.

Her name was Buttercup but I was determined to morph this cow into a horse called Trigger. It was a long summer — a battle of wills. It took weeks just to get Trigger to let me mount her from the barnyard fence. It was even longer before she would move in ANY direction after I was on her back. Some days I made progress and other days she was simply a stupid cow. I began every morning with renewed determination, trying this and trying that until one magic morning, my pal Trigger moseyed me down the cow path to bring home the cows.

I'll never know what that cow thought of our summer accomplishments, but for me that summer I discovered something that has guided me all my life . . . the power of Da Um Jeitinho . . . there is always a way!

~ by Bernajean Porter

By taking time to reflect upon your life experiences and perhaps being willing to enhance or restructure your story from a new perspective, the story will enable you to heal or redefine the path you walk. Even the simple act of searching the multitude of possible personal stories to tell allows you to sort, prioritize and finally select one life experience that represents something especially important to you in the here and now. Each digital story uses a personal experience to develop a living memory with a specific point, a moral, an a-ha awareness or a specific understanding. And just think of the joy and insights your life story will give to all those who know you and all those who are yet to know you in future time.

Kinship Stories: Family Stories of Who We Are

We can all claim colorful, adventurous, crazy, loving, well-meaning, shameless, mysterious, frightening, funny or influential family members. Some kinship stories have become legends in families and others have sadly been lost through time. Every family has a hidden closet of a few relatives they would rather not claim – even these stories can provide a perspective of family dynamics.

Unless you are supporting a family member to tell their own digital story, it is important to use the kinship stories as a vehicle to develop your own story. Rather than telling a story about a family member, consider using that same story or experience to reveal a personal point-of-view of your own. Family stories become the foundation of telling something about who we are. While it may enrich the kinship story to weave in a family member's vocal perspective as a supporting "guest voice," the story script/voiceover itself needs to be your own. How does some family story touch you personally? How did having that family member in your life affect you? In what ways did hearing the story of a relative or family experience shape your values or your own choices? What lessons did you learn? What personal meaning did the family stories make for your own life?

Every life is a story like a thread that interweaves with myriads of others to form a tapestry of humanity.

~ Michael Roemer

In every conceivable
manner, the family is link
to our past, bridge to
our future.

~ Alex Haley

Kinship Story Ideas

- A family folklore – tall tales or exaggerated, silly stories about
  relatives long ago
- A story of courage
- A story about family names
- A story of strength
- An infamous relative
- A story of pride
- A story of lost or found family members
- A story of determination
- A story of fortunes lost or found
- A story of historical events that changed or influenced the family
- A story of heirlooms
- A family tradition passed down to you
- A story of family recipes
- A family mystery
- A story of family holidays
- A visit or memory of the place of family origin
- A story of adopted family members
- A memory piece in response to a family photo
- An imagined story invented from an
  unlabeled family photo
- Compare and contrast your life today
  with a past family member's life

Hyper-Interactive Stories: Group Stories with Diverse Paths and Endings

Most stories experienced through time thus far were crafted for listeners to receive and enjoy. The nature of telling or writing structured stories was generally linear usually by a single author in response to a specific audience. The art and talent belonged to the storyteller rather than the listener. Then arrived the choose-your-own-adventure or twist-a-plot books that began to change the idea of the author being in complete control of the actions and story line.

These interactive books were organized around letting a reader encounter a series of situations or story points with either a real or imagined story plot. The author then presented choices at each story point by inviting the readers to make their own decisions of what happens next. For example, if you want to jump into a hole, turn to page 12. If you want to climb the tree, turn to page 23. If you want to go back into the rainforest, turn to page 9. These choose-your-own adventure stories unfolded multiple story paths and endings but still depended upon the choices only the authors developed for their reader. Giving the storyline choices in this way to readers did begin to share the storytelling thereby increasing the engagement and enjoyment by many readers in novel ways.

Now such emerging mediums as computers, Internet, personal websites, and hypermedia software enable storytellers to extend beyond the printed modes of choose-your-own-adventures. Hyper-interactive stories now allow readers or users to jump to new story paths by clicking rather than turning to a specific page to pick up their story path. We are still creatively inventing this new story type and exploring its possibilities with a variety of names: hyperfiction, collaborative literature, hypertext, twist-adventures and hyperstories.

This category of digital story is still playfully emerging from primarily text formats to text with images but awaiting even more invention and experimenting with future movie-like vignettes. Because of the newness of hyper-interac-

> Hypertext, which links one block of text or ideas to a myriad others, destroys [the] physical isolation of the text, just as it also destroys the attitudes created by that isolation.
>
> ~ George P. Landow

tive stories, it is worth taking a bit of time here to spark imaginations to experiment with other digital forms not yet common but on the horizon. Four general qualities make hyper-interactive stories unique from oral or printed stories: **collaborative story writing**, **media rich tales**, **hyper-linking**, and **digital sharing**.

1. Collaborative story writing using multiple authors can take two approaches to hyper-interactive story telling: closed or open. Closed collaborative stories are organized closer to the present choose-your-own-adventure books. They have planned beginnings, paths and endings that everyone contributes to developing but are not open to ongoing change. Family or student groups might work together organizing their real or imagined story structure by co-creating a flow chart of the varied links or paths. The various story paths are then developed by different or multiple authors. For example, students might divide among themselves the creating of a hyper-interactive tour of the human body telling the personal story of the importance of each body function. Families might divide up the storytelling of their family tree using a twist-a-plot adventure.

Open collaborative writings begin with a storyline that first lets users make choices within the story paths of others. But then, users are encouraged to write/add new choices of their own wherever, whenever they like. The tales grow and change over time with new story paths. These open collaborative stories become literally neverending stories with hundreds of paths and endings written by any and all who join in. Each page of the story is unique, and can lead to others as the user chooses. And those, in turn, can lead to others, which, in turn, can lead to even more... and so the story goes on forever. Collaborative writings that are publicly posted are generally organized around a common theme and expected to use family-acceptable vocabulary and graphics.

2. Media rich hyper-interactive stories are based on earlier choose-your-own adventure books that were obviously text-based with few, if any, illustrations.

Hypertext creates a constellation of ideas ... that can be reached by electronic, digital communication, anywhere on the planet.

~ Christopher Nash

Many of the present Web-based hyper-interactive stories are still text driven as well. However, these new digital interactive stories can easily go beyond hypertext by creating media rich stories that incorporate images, graphics, sound and motion. New and presently edgy software with higher learning curves continues to emerge enabling the creation of multimedia rich stories, which can be posted for a worldwide audience.

New software tools let storywriters "write" outside the traditional linear text box. Rather than being considered "pages" to write upon and read, a few new software tools allow groups to create "scenes" that are directed by and inter-acted with by other users. These scenes can include voiceover, images, etc. The software also supports easy Web publishing and interacting with stories creat-ed online. Try exploring some of these new software tools: *mPower5* (mmde-sign.com), *Kahootz* (kahootz.com) or *QTI* (ezedia.com).

Authors can now also use new software designed to create "hot spots" or hyperlinks onto their video clips letting users interact with additional informa-tion or ideas. Try exploring videoclix.com, which is presently a professional tool but expected to enter the mainstream in the near future. Or think about what a hyper-interactive story would literally look like if collaborative groups created virtual reality environments with 360 degree images and hot links into other spaces. Many, many new products are emerging that enable authors to visually design and express concepts, experiences and other worlds for users to interact with in unique ways. The software plus our imagination will — over time — make new possibilities not even mentioned in this book.

I could link a million ways but it will take some time too think it through.

~ J. Nathan Matias

3. Hyperlinking is a form of non-linear navigation designed into stories to give choices to the users. This technical function of "hot links" has become a trade-mark of digital environments. Links can be designed into text and images that when clicked allow users control in jumping to other places, going deeper into details or connecting to related information of their choice. This feature is per-fect for making links that enable users to make personal choices to take differ-ent story paths. Because of our long ingrained experience with linear stories

Sample Hyper-Interactive Web Sites

There is an abundance of interactive story websites covering many themes. Be careful to filter any sites used as many of them have violent or sexual content. Use sites that expect family-friendly content and monitor their story postings to ensure they are using family-oriented or G-rated material. Here are a few sites to consider:

- HeroQuest is an online, interactive adventure, in which YOU are both the hero and the story-teller. As you encounter a situation, you are presented with choices on what to do with it—choices that could lead to victory, or defeat. Trust yourself, and see if you can become a hero! Begin your journey! (www.digifort.com/heroquest/)

- The Story Sprawl is a hyperfiction Website that also features their stories in MP3 audio dramatizations. (www.storysprawl.com/)

- Choose-Your-Own-Adventure's site provides a story generator to read and write your own hyper-interactive books. Some of the features that make this site stand out from the rest are writing clans, image uploads, public/private story rooms, approval system, private messaging, and room linking. (www.choose-your-own-adventure.com)

- NeverEnding Tales is intended for the "young at heart." They ask for the content of the stories to be created MOSTLY (75%) by kids, and PARTLY (25% or less) by older teens and adults. History with a Twist and The Magic Scroll of 3000 Books are samples of fun and intellectual themes that invite the interplay of imagination and learning. (www.coder.com/creations/tale/)

Hyper-Interactive Story Ideas

- Organize a kinship storytelling project to engage multiple family members in sharing the family's history through the ages, or relate multiple versions of a common family event.
- Create a twist-a-plot with multiple endings or alternative actions for a historical or current event issue.
- Create a choose-your-own-adventure using fictional plots, tall tales or myths.
- Create an authentic twist-a-plot tour with multiple time periods explored – organize the choices with the metaphor of time machines or magical caves or black holes that can open the portals of time.
- Create choose-your-own-adventure tours of non-fiction information – tours of states, countries, brains, planets, etc.
- Create twist-a-plots using fictional or non-fictional topics to present multiple points of view or varied historical perspectives. For example, Paul Revere, George Washington, a slave, an indentured servant, King George or varied Indian tribes are shadowed through key events in the Revolutionary War.
- Create twist-a-plots using a current event topic viewed through multiple cultural perspectives such as American, European, South African, etc.

and technologies, stories using hyperlinking need more up front navigational structure so users do not get lost. Storyboarding usually takes the form of flow-charts to organize the multiple story paths. Organizing these interactive stories can be logistically challenging. If your stories are mostly text-based, consider subscribing to a special adventure story engine open to public and private writing groups found at www.choose-your-own-adventure.com. Here you will be able to participate in posted adventure stories or begin your own hyper-story room for private group participation using their software engine to organize all the branching.

4. Digital sharing via Websites enables stories to be posted and shared literally with the world. No longer are collaborative writing groups artificially constrained by the physical distance between authors and users. With a little organization and a web page, students, families and others can easily create stories together. Not only does digital sharing enable groups to work together but it also provides a unique way to share their stories with strangers whom they have yet to meet.

Personal Expression: Creating Visual Expressions of Thoughts and Feelings

Personal Expression refers to a type of communication in which the author expresses a subjective and introspective message. Original poetry, visual interpretations, montages, or topical reflections for example, would be personal expression. Personal Expression communication does not involve an attempt to persuade or convince an audience directly of a perspective or point of view; instead, it shares and many times influences an audience through expressing the author's experiences, feelings, or point of view of complex and/or emotional ideas. These digital stories invite the imagination to construct varied types of free-form expressions of original thought. All preconceived constraints are lifted. Authors are challenged to experiment with the medium and message in non-traditional ways.

Personal Expression Story Ideas

- Interpret an existing poem that touches your life with voice, images and sound.
- Create an interpretive visual story on a historic, personal or current event.
- Create a group text poem that each individual then translates into a personal visual/sound expression.
- Choose and relate a montage of photos or images or sounds that shares feelings and thoughts on personal, historical, current event, or reflective topics.
- Create and interpret your own poem on a special topic – a trip, a current event, a historical character or event, a clash in world values, or a hero who influenced your life.

Storytelling reveals meaning without committing the error of defining it.

~ Hannah Arendt

Myths, Legends and Tales: Past, Present, and Future

Myths are stories made up by people to explain their origins, values, and beliefs. The author may tell an established myth, such as the mythical Greek story of Prometheus or the Navaho creation myth. Myths can also include stories made up by the author but having myth-like qualities. An author may, for example, invent a myth-like story to explain the origin of a family heirloom.

Of course it's true, but it may not have happened.

~ Patricia Polacco's Grandmother

Legends are stories of an inspiring person, feat or achievement. These people or achievements are deemed worthy or enduring. Legends are generally considered real and often represent renowned historical characters or events. But many times when legends pass through generations by word of mouth, story parts are added that cannot always be proven as literal happenings. These stories often include romanticized and embellished details developed over time

Myths, Legends, and Tales Story Ideas

- Investigate and translate an ancient legend into a modern tale.
- Create a myth about your own life.
- Develop myths from "what would happen if."
- Create myths of "how things came to be" in your life, school or business
- Change a current event into a tall tale or myth.
- Develop a legend of a family member's life or accomplishment.
- Create a legend of your own life for your great, great grandchildren to pass on.
- Create a fractured fairy tale.
- Create tall tales of inventing something for the future.

to strengthen the legend's importance to others. Most families and organizations have generated some legends that are passed onto the new generations as models or examples that represent values and pride.

Folk tales are similar to myths and legends in that they tell stories which have been developed and modified by groups of people over periods of time. Usually license has been taken to exaggerate the event or person in playful ways in order to make a point. The Johnny Appleseed or Paul Bunyan stories are examples of American folk tales. There are many, many folk tales from all places and cultures in the world. An author may choose to visually re-interpret an established folk tale or may invent a folk tale-like story about a family member, a product, or an accomplishment of their own.

While most myths, legends or folktales are passed down to us through generations as oral and written stories, their unique style can also be applied to present and future people and events. For example, create a legend or tall tale about the future things you might do with your life leaving this digital story "behind" for great, great grandchildren. Enjoy the playfulness of creating personal digital stories with the myth, legend and tall tales perspective.

Informative or Expository Stories: Information Beyond Words

Informative / Expository stories presume that factual concepts, ideas or information learned contain useful material, ideas and concepts to communicate to others. These forms include summary reports, biographies, book reports, etc. They do not attempt to persuade audience members of any perspective, point

Informative or Expository Story Ideas

- Create a personal reflection on something learned.
- Create biographies of family members.
- Create biographies of famous or important people.
- Create biographies of inanimate objects or situations demonstrating essential information.
- Provide "How-to" directions to teach a specialty or something newly learned.
- Explain an "aha" or understanding.
- Summarize information and how you think or feel about the topic.
- Share the experience and reactions of a book read.
- Share the experience and reactions of a historical event's impact.

The main part of intellectual education is not the acquisition of facts but learning how to make facts live.

~ Oliver Wendell Holmes

of view, or plan of action. The information / expository forms of communication involve explanations that can now go beyond words to actually construct visual models, animated demonstrations, and sensory understandings that "show" rather than "tell" about concepts learned. The use of a narrative voice developed with a "script" for these digital stories reflects the author's full intellectual and personal engagement with the subject — not just a reporting of facts and information. While this category is likely to be more suited for students to express their learning of information beyond text reports, exemplar communication of information is an essential skill for all ages. Storytellers practice the art of translating raw information into valuable knowledge from their own crystallized perspective within a memorable digital story.

Persuasive Stories: Influencing and Impacting Others

When an author creates persuasive communications, a conscious attempt is made to persuade the audience to share the same point of view or belief as the author. We are constantly inundated with media generating their messages to influence us in our thinking and choices. In all communication arenas — commercial, political, religious, movie making, and community flyers — more than words are being used to persuade us. Consumers now need conscious understanding of how color, images, symbols, voice tones, music and pacing of these persuasive messages influence us. There is no better way than to engage in and practice being designers of information that uses multimedia intentionally to influence and impact others. By being inside the design process of scripting and choosing various visual and sound elements, we become conscious of techniques used by others to persuade. Adults, especially teachers, need this experience as much as students do.

Persuasive forms include public service announcements, advertisements, and other communication types that challenge us to describe/conclude, analyze/persuade, analyze/conclude, compare/contrast, or show cause/effect.

```
╔══════════════════════════════════════════════╗
║  Persuasive Story Ideas                        ║
║                                                ║
║  • Compare and contrast a past event with a present event. ║
║  • Relate a cause and effect situation or dilemma.         ║
║  • Create an analysis and conclusion of an unresolved topic. ║
║  • Create an advertisement to influence or shape opinions on issues. ║
║  • Create a public service spot that persuades others to take action. ║
║  • Create a brief documentary for topics that describe and conclude. ║
╚══════════════════════════════════════════════╝
```

It is essential that the intent to persuade is an inherent component of the structure of this type of digital story using the power of voice, music and images to influence and impact. Persuasive stories must communicate complex ideas and at the same time create their impact quickly. In persuasion the author uses, either singly or in combination, any of a battery of tools to sway the audience through an intellectual appeal, an emotional appeal, or both. Some television commercials, for example, attempt to sell us a product by showing images that suggest that people who buy their product will have happy family members by using warm, pleasant settings, while people who don't buy the product are portrayed as unhappy and alone. Here they used emotional appeal. On the other hand, political commercials comparing and contrasting two candidates' views on medical care might argue their case based on an intellectual appeal. The art of designing and communicating information that is useful and beneficial to others needs to be explicitly practiced in an age of information.

Itza Wrap: Telling Digital Stories of Lessons Learned

Itza Wrap is a variation of digital storytelling expressing personal narratives/experiences about lessons learned from projects, initiatives, grants or units of study. They are reflective stories that reveal personal experiences and

The principal goal of education is to create people who are capable of doing (and thinking) new things, not simply repeating what other generations have done.

~ Piaget

He who knows not his own genius has none.

~ William Blake

answer the questions what did you hear? What did you learn? And what do you think? What insight(s) did the experience give you? What do you now know or understand? Itza Wrap stories showcase personal experiences in grants, goals, initiatives and special projects, add compelling human experience to text/numeric evaluations or action research projects, or create personal reflections for student/teacher portfolios on lessons learned.

Roger Schanks, known for his work in artificial intelligence, comments that "learning from one's own experiences depends upon being able to communicate our experiences as stories to others." This category of stories has more to do with conveying the emotional, inspiring and qualitative value of experience rather than conveying specific information about content or program logistics or summarizing details. Digital storytelling at the end of projects, programs or initiatives engages each person's voice in telling the personal story of lessons learned using their own unique experiences. Itza Wrap digital stories honor the work and learning of the participants, as well as inspiring others in ways that data cannot. These digital stories require participants to answer some very important questions for themselves and others: What difference did we make? What difference can the work or learning we develop continue to make for others?

The personal narrative of an Itza Wrap digital story is organized around three main plot points: context, experience and impact.

• The first plot point identifies the context of the project for the viewer. What was the title and purpose(s)? What results and outcomes were expected? For whom? Do not take up too much story space telling project information or implementation logistics – this is not directly about knowing the project. We need to know only enough to give the context for your story. Consider context as similar to a story's setting.

• The second plot point describes your personal experience. Where did you start in your beliefs, skills or attitudes? What were the key highlights or learn-

Itza Wrap Story Ideas

Students and teachers create portfolio stories:

- Express understanding and application of concepts learned from a unit of study
- Reflect on themselves as learners from a semester class
- Describe key topical concepts, weaving together why each was chosen and what personal meaning they have
- Create a story of lessons learned from a challenging unit

School staff creates stories for publicity, web sites and local news:

- Teachers create a story of the impact of a grant on their students
- Team leaders summarize the journey of initiating and launching a pilot program or project
- Teachers provide stories that demonstrate findings in evaluation projects

Communities, business and organizations create stories for publicity, websites, presentations, and communications:

- Churches gather membership stories about faith experiences
- Businesses gather employee stories about special initiatives or projects
- Businesses gather client stories about customer satisfaction
- Schools gather parents/student stories about their experiences with initiatives or programs
- Organizations gather membership stories about their impact and accomplishments
- Summer camps gather stories of experiences that represent the value of participating
- Special events gather stories of personal experiences that reflect on the successes

An Itza Wrap Story Script: The Music In My Head

The music in my head was always there, but I had not yet discovered the instrument. I was a different kind of teacher even before eMINTS. I was one of those teachers you worried about from the day you hired me. I carried with me a strange bag of experiences ranging from sailing off the coast of Florida with 14 Attention Deficit Children, to catching frogs in a swamp with a group of students from a private school in New York City. I could feel the invisible walls everywhere I went. Sometimes it bothered me to be so different from the others, but every once in a while someone would hear the music in my head, and we would both smile. eMINTS came along, and suddenly I realized I had discovered my instrument. The music in my head was not my music, it belonged to my students. I became the conductor of a huge orchestra of learning. eMINTS showed me how to give my students the freedom to guide their own learning. Soon the music was being heard by others, though they were not sure where it was coming from. I had found my instrument, the one that everyone could hear. The one that could fit in. The one that others wanted to learn how to play. The more I practice eMINTS, the better I become. The music draws other teachers like the pied piper. Everyone wants to hear the music that eMINTS has given me. The walls dissolve, the music plays, and I will never be the same kind of teacher again.

Amber was a student in my class during my first year of eMINTS. She was one of those students you worry about from the day they walk into your room. She carried with her the anger, attitude, and reputation that had been dealt to her in this small community of learners. You could feel the invisible walls around her everywhere she went. Sometimes it bothered her to be so different from the others, but every once in a while she would show me the music in her head and we would both smile. I started to listen hard for that music, and encouraged her to listen too. Amber had a special way of playing her music that was out of tune for everyone else. She had a hard time packaging herself and her ideas in a way that could be accepted by her peers. How could she let them into her world? That gift came in eMINTS wrapping. She unwrapped her instrument and began to make beautiful music with it. Soon the music was being heard by others, though they were not sure where it was coming from. Amber could take a task and turn it into something that no other student would have dreamed. The more open-ended my teaching became, the louder her music played. Soon her music was impossible to ignore. It drew the other students to her like the pied piper. Everyone wanted to be a part of her musical. The walls dissolved, the music played, and Amber changed her world. She will never be the same kind of student again. The music in her head was always there, but she had not yet discovered the instrument. ~ by Amy Vejraska

ing experiences? There isn't time to include everything that happened – find the part in the story that will quickly represent the essence of your experience. Consider experience similar to a story's plot.

• The third plot point reveals the impact or difference that was made – the lesson(s) learned. This is the key message that makes up a major portion of the emotional space if not story space. Understanding "impact" should not be an afterthought or post script – it is the heart of the story for the author as well as the viewers. The Itza Wrap story is organized around sharing the impact. Design visual representations, sound, the use of "guest voice(s)" and other digital compositions to evoke understanding, inspiration and appreciation for lessons learned – the differences that were made. Consider impact as similar to a story's dénouement

Whether in businesses, organizations or schools, the power of people's work and experiences is much greater than the numbers found in evaluations or bottom lines. Any individual, non-profit organization or business that wants to generate publicity or even build community within their project groups will find personal digital stories of their work worth doing and probably even more powerful than sending out a professional camera crew to try to capture their stories.

Future Vision Stories: Imagining the Future NOW

Building shared visions begins with individual visions. Knowing your own dreams of what you want is deeply satisfying and fulfilling. Aligning these individual visions within organizations creates a vibrant experience that collectively shapes everyone's possibilities. Peter Senge, author of *Fifth Discipline*, points out that traditional models of centralizing power and authority at the top are becoming increasingly dysfunctional. An individual or organization's vision should live deep in heart of the individual's or organization members' values and cannot be dictated by others.

Take time to gather up the past so that you will be able to draw from your experiences and invest them in the future.

~ Jim Rohn

Visioning implies that individuals, organizations or businesses are moving into a way of life or doing business not presently happening. Real change means inventing and implementing together. Margaret Wheatley, author of *Leadership and the New Science*, finds that "the clearer the image of the destination, the more force the future image exerts on the present, pulling us into that desired future state." She defines vision as an energy field or force that needs to permeate through the entire organization. This vision energy field (aka morphogenic field) influences and shapes behaviors to become congruent with the organization's goals. So the more real we can make the imagined, the more clarity we can imagine, the more emotionally attached we become to the new views, then the more the new idea moves into reality.

Digital stories let us become our own directors rolling out our imagined visions in colorful, image-full movies. These digital stories help visions come alive in our hearts almost literally with animated, positive multi-sensory images that engage everyone's emotions. Our blank screens about what the future looks like become filled with moving images, sound and personal narratives.

Creating the type of digital story called Future Visions is a process that develops vivid scenarios. Future Visions was also discussed in *Chapter 1: And That Reminds Me of A Story That Needs to Be Told* as one of the powers of story-

> In times of change, learners inherit the Earth, while the learned find themselves beautifully equipped to deal with a world that no longer exists.
>
> ~ Eric Hoffer

> The best thing about the future is that it only comes one day at a time.
>
> ~ Abraham Lincoln

Elements of a Future Vision Story

- A desired future expresses our best hopes 7+ years from now.
- Use images, sounds and narrative details that show (not tell) a day in the life of one person who might be expected to be part of this future – yourself, a student, a parent, a customer.
- Embed values and qualities of the most desired future.
- Use first person to make it more intimate and real.
- Speak in the present tense as if the future is already happening.

Future Vision Story Ideas

Individual Visions:

- What would you do if you knew you could not fail?
- Write a short story that portrays in first person an imagined future AS IF it already exists.
- Suppose you had a vision of greatness . . . what would that be?
- Imagine achieving the results in your life that you deeply desire. What would it look and feel like?
- If you could be exactly the person you would want to be, what would be your qualities? What would you be doing with your life?
- Imagine your life has a unique purpose . . . describe your work, your relationships or some aspect of your life AS IF you were NOW living a life that reflected your purpose.

Community and Organization Visions:

- Tell a story that demonstrates new values and ways of working together AS IF we are all living in that new story NOW.
- What is your vision for the community you live in?
- Create stories with all the details of living NOW in neighborhoods, schools,o. or organizations AS IF they have already transformed themselves.
- Create a story that solves a problem AS IF that solution is working perfectly.

telling. Future visions tell the story of a day in the life of someone living the invented story in first person. These stories are told in present tense as if they were already real. Out of all the probabilities, the most desired future is imagined and activated by imagining it is already so in great, rich detail so it can be brought to life. When large groups create multiple scenarios, they identify the common qualities found in their stories. These common qualities form the basis for vision statements. But the stories continue to influence individuals, organizations and communities beyond the actual vision statement words by showing rather than telling.

Visioning is powerful, mighty and potent when we consciously focus on the desired outcomes of our best hopes. Consider co-creating a common vision by holding town-meetings, future searches, or other large group gatherings to identify future directions together. I have personally facilitated numerous events that developed scenarios as a way of inventing the future. This intensive process of involving large groups in making future vision digital stories takes considerably more time than many visioning processes, but it also increases the speed and depth of moving visions into actual practice. The more people involved, the faster the gap between the vision and today's reality is closed according to the experiences of Robert Jacobs, author of *Real-time Strategic Change*. Groups who use digital storytelling to create future visions will quickly fill their personal and organization's energy fields with clarity, commitment, and urgency to make "it" real.

My will shall shape the future. Whether I fail or succeed only I hold the key to my destiny.

~ Elaine Maxwell

Where there is no hope in the future, there is no power in the present. ~ John Maxwell

~ John Maxwell

Sample Future Vision Story

Here is a sample future vision story I facilitated with five regional community meetings, almost 1500 participants including students, for Denver Public Schools. At all community meetings, groups of four to five participants created personal stories to answer the question "What would a day in the life of a DPS student look like seven years from now when their best hopes for technology and learning combined with student skills needed for success in a changing world came together in ways that worked for them?" Common qualities were identified from all the stories making sure they were possible and obtainable. The following scenarios represent one version of the new stories that Denver Public Schools expected to tell when the vision for technology and learning was implemented. Imagine translating this text story into the power of a digital story that is posted and circulated among any staff and community who were not present at the meetings!

My name is Pat. I am in the fourth grade. On the way out of the door, I grab my backpack and laptop. All of my homework and research is on my laptop. I am taking it to school.

When I arrive at school I grab a cup of hot chocolate and meet with my interaction group. We discuss issues, present projects, ask questions, talk about interests, and our digital goal stories. I shared some great resources found on the Internet last night. We love to start our day in the school coffeeshop atmosphere.

I then move on to my special interest group. Today I first go to my collaboration research group. We are investigating issues/solutions for raising the standard of living in Africa. We pull up information on the Internet to locate a pen-pal school in Africa to help us gather local information. After turning on the automatic translator, we discuss issues and interests with other fourth grade students in a school in Nairobi. We work together with our new friends in completing our report on a possible solution. It will have local photographs, video clips and special music composed by our email classmates in Africa. We wrap up the video presentation for tomorrow and head out to our next groups. I am working on new music goals that include

learning the synthesizer to compose a new school song that I want to submit to our student council.

After lunch, it is time for my favorite part of the day, our digital communication arts group. I am beginning a new language arts/social studies project called Columbus, The Devil or Discoverer. My teacher comes over to make sure that I am on the right track. She helps me generate a mind-map of the questions and information I need to gather in order to develop my documentary. She suggests I go to the Internet to pull up some other perspectives regarding this issue. I am working on efficient searches with the new visual search engines we learned this spring.

And then it is time to switch over to my Chinese class. I hook up to my distance learning with my Chinese professor who is televising from Beijing. We are concentrating on Mandarin. It helps to have voice recognition software to visually see my pronunciations. I finally get to go to my late afternoon break. It is so nice to go swimming with my friend. I love the new forty-foot water slide. Tonight I will work on the math problem I signed up for that will figure out how much chlorine is needed for our new pool per month.

Chapter 5

Stepping Through Making a Digital Story

The novelty and technical fun of multimedia can sometimes divert and endanger the quality of the story. When the digital storytelling is finished, you want your story to be remembered for its soul, not the bells and whistles.

~ Bernajean Porter

Crafting a Digital Story

This is an overview for crafting your digital stories. Seven process steps and resources are outlined within four production phases to guide you in developing all types of digital stories. Creating digital stories adds more dimensions to traditional story-making as well as dealing with a multitude of challenges: finding your own inner stories; the scary thrill of tapping into personal creativity; learning an array of software and hardware tools; designing and creating with digital tools; and the inevitable — time management.

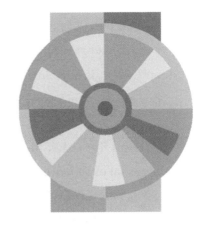

Rather than learning all these areas before getting started, it is recommended that digital storytellers work in groups whether you are doing an individual story or creating a team story. The storytelling needs of the script (personal narrative story) drive the scope of technical functions necessary to learn for each project. As you identify the story project's technical needs, the varied tasks can be divided up among group members to learn whatever is needed to complete the work. Learning what you need when you need it is called just-in-time learning, which provides the kind of context that anchors learning of a multitude of technical and design skills. Because there are so many ways to express your creativeness, you will likely find it both joyful and challenging to have so many options and possibilities in developing your story. These story-making steps make it easy to engage in the all the learning processes required to take you from a great idea to a fully developed digital story.

While there are a multitude of design guidelines that professionals have spent years learning, the best practice is to mimic what you like. It is highly recommended before starting your own project to have fun watching many examples of digital stories. Take note of techniques and story elements that you find engaging and appealing. Also take note of any distracting storytelling styles or technical approaches that you want to be sure NOT to replicate.

If you are the same person after reading a book, seeing a picture, hearing music, then what you read, saw or heard was not produced by an artist.

~ Robert Burdette Sweet, The Writer as Shaman.

Viewing Digital Stories Around the World

Here are sample websites for viewing online video examples of digital storytelling. They will give you an overview of personal digital storytelling from many points of view. As you browse these examples, consider what is appealing about the way each story unfolds, what techniques were used effectively, and what, if anything, you would advise yourself NOT to do with the story you are making. Be curious about what makes these stories powerful.

• **The DigiTales Story Keepers Gallery** is a collection of living memories, lessons learned and personal experiences with ideas developed as digital stories. These were created by kids and adults who participated in DigiTales Storytelling Camps. They left knowing the better part of who they and others can be through their stories. (www.digitales.us)

• **The Center for Digital Storytelling** is a non-profit project dedicated to assisting people in using digital media to tell meaningful stories from their lives. Their focus is on developing large-scale projects for community, educational and business institutions. (www.storycenter.org)

• **Next Exit** is an interactive theatrical performance created and presented by Dana Atchley, who sits on a log next to a digital campfire and, drawing from a virtual suitcase of seventy stories, creates a unique selection for each audience. (www.nextexit.com/nextexit/showframeset.html)

• **Telling LIVES** is a non-profit project with the BBC inviting teenagers, World War II veterans, and ordinary people from England to tell their stories. (www.bbc.co.uk/tellinglives)

• **Island Movies** are stories from a digital storytelling contest for students in Hawaii, Alaska and Japan. Students demonstrate their creative writing, collaborative teamwork, and digital movie-making skills. Based on curriculum with a content focus, the videos display what students know, care about, and are able to do in understanding the unique and significant aspects of their cultures. (www.islandmovie.k12.hi.us)

• **Capturing Wales** is another BBC project that shows the richness of life in Wales through stories made by the people of Wales. Monthly public workshops around Wales are held to help citizens create their own digital stories. (www.bbc.co.uk/wales/capturewales)

Overview of Four Phases of Digital StoryMaking

The process of making a digital story can be organized into four separate (and sometimes overlapping) phases. Anyone who has learned the stages of writing will feel comfortable with working in these progressive phases. Get set to learn a lot of new vocabulary as many of the terms are borrowed from the professional filmmaking world. Creating personal digital stories originated with Joe Lambert, Director of the Center for Digital Storytelling. Lambert adapted and merged elements from the stage, film and storytelling worlds. (www.storycenter.org) Joe dedicates his work to the memory of his friend Dana Atchley, media artist, producer and performer who inspired the idea of collecting memories in the format of digital media. (www.nextexit.com/nextexit/nextframeset.html). Each of the four phases has separate process steps of tasks for story and technical development of a digital movie. Using these phases and steps will pace the learning and work for success.

> I've always tried to be aware of what I say in my films, because all of us who make motion pictures are teachers; teachers with very loud voices.
>
> ~ George Lucas

Pre-production Phase

This is the development and planning phase. Every story starts with an idea. The ideas are explored, refined and organized using planning tools like scripts and storyboards. You will be completing the first three process steps during the pre-production phase: **Writing** a narrative script; **planning** the project with storyboards and creating shot and sound lists; and **organizing** the project folders to sort the resources as you create them.

Production Phase

After the planning is completed during the pre-production phase, it is time for the production phase of gathering and preparing all media elements. Producing includes recording, filming, downloading files from the Internet or digitizing the images, artifacts, sound, and other media elements needed to tell the story. This takes as much time as it takes. However, the image and sound lists made in the pre-production phase will guide you in making decisions about how many media resources are really needed. *See Chapter 7: Entering the Technical World of Digital Media* for more technical details for production skills. The production phase has two process steps: **Making** the voiceover and **gathering** the media resources.

Post-Production Phase

This phase involves merging and editing the media resources into a finished, ready-to-view digital movie. It includes a lot of creative technical work that will have more flow if the previous steps have been completed. Video editing software programs *(iMovie, Final Cut, Ulead's VideoStudio 8, or Premiere)* may vary but their approach and functions are similar. Just like using a word processor, certain operating functions can be expected in these programs regardless of the software name. However, there are some vendors who claim their product can be used for video editing when in reality it doesn't include the full range of tools you need. It is frustrating to need additional programs that require another investment of time to learn how to use them. *See Chapter 6: Poof! Creating a DigiTales Toolkit* to consider the tools that are right for you. The post-production phase has one process step: **Putting** IT all together.

Distribution Phase

Even though the digital movie is technically finished, there is still one more essential phase: sharing the final digital story! This phase encourages the celebration of the ideas, messages, and creative energy of your digital stories with friends, family, co-workers or strangers far and wide. What playback or publishing format(s) will you find most useful? Most but not all video editing tools allow authors to export their story in multiple formats. Depending on your software and hardware tools, you can choose to publish in only one format or make a variety of formats. *See Chapter 7: Entering the Technical World of*

Editing (film) is visual poetry.

~ George Lucas

Digital Media for additional technical support of file formats. The distribution phase has one process step: **Applause! Applause!**

Overview of Seven Process Steps for StoryMaking

For those who have experienced process writing as a series of steps from brainstorming to finished product, you can also think of digital storytelling as a series of process steps from start to finish. Seven process steps are outlined within the four phases of production to help you organize successful individual or group projects. The process steps in this section are general guidelines with suggestions, tips, strategies and resources.

Regardless of your audiences or purposes, feel free to vary, mix or match, modify or invent according to your own personal choice and style. After all the guidelines, steps and rules-of-thumb, the most important element of a successful digital story is to have fun! May these seven process steps help you translate your imagination and talents into a story you will be proud to tell!

Seven Process Steps to Digital Storytelling

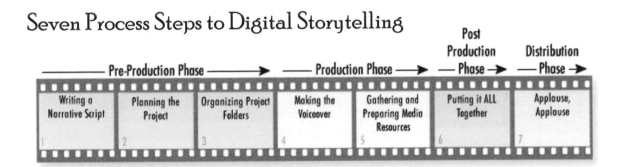

Pre-Production Phase			Production Phase		Post Production Phase	Distribution Phase
Writing a Narrative Script	Planning the Project	Organizing Project Folders	Making the Voiceover	Gathering and Preparing Media Resources	Putting it ALL Together	Applause, Applause
1	2	3	4	5	6	7

Step 1. Writing a Narrative Script (Pre-production Phase)

A digital storytelling script is a first person narrative that tells the story in your own voice and style. Unlike the making of a film documentary, the written script is the heart and soul of the digital story organizing all the other media elements. Before writing the script, you will want to find your story.

Brainstorm story ideas. Be clear about your purpose, audience and where the final product will be viewed. Remember, if it can be written or thought, it can be made into a digital story. The narrative script is captured later as a voiceover during the production stage.

Choosing Your Story

One of the most unique features of this specific digital storytelling style is the expectation that each story expresses a personal meaning or insight. Using personal mementos, artifacts, and a variety of multimedia, digital storytelling unfolds as a personal story. It is not about other people. It is not simply telling about the event or situation. Whatever story you choose to make into a digital story, the written script needs to be about how this particular story touched your own life. The development of this feature originated with Dana Atchley and Joe Lambert. The process of identifying and creating this kind of digital story provides a profound experience for both new and experienced storytellers. Reflect on the following questions to help develop a story that speaks to you:

- What type of story catches your imagination and sense of fun?
- What story idea from the brainstorming has interest and passion for you?
- What makes this story worth doing?

While some storytellers are able to face a blank page or screen with ease, others find the task frustrating and often feel extremely vulnerable. Some stories start with pictures or images. Others start in the heart. Good stories have insight. While searching for your story, let your mind play with ideas, trusting that you will instinctively know and be inspired by the story that needs to be told. If you are looking for ideas, browse and consider the suggestions in *Chapter 4: Conjuring Up Stories Ideas.*

Drafting the Written Script

Once you have chosen your story idea, it is time to begin generating your story plot ideas and drafting a written script. All stories have a structure. Even a short story has a beginning, an end and uses a thread of events to hold it together. A good digital story has a destination – a point to make – and seeks the shortest path to its destination. It holds creative tension for the viewer – a burning question of some kind that is sustained until the end. And then the author finally reveals the moral of the story, the lesson learned or an understanding gained from the story. The key point or moral that you make with your story can be implicitly or explicitly stated with words or images. Take time to review and consider *Take Six: Elements of a Good Story* considered fundamental to developing this particular digital storytelling style BEFORE you brainstorm your story plot ideas:

- Living inside your story
- Unfolding lessons learned
- Developing creative tension
- Economizing the storyline
- Showing not telling
- Demonstrating craftsmanship

TIP: Take time to consider the *Take Six: Elements of a Good Story* (p.116) before drafting your story script. Embedding these elements will move ordinary tales into memorable enduring stories.

TIP: Target drafting no more than a one-page script using 500 words or LESS as the length for an approximate 3 to 5 minute finished digital story.

TIP: Try generating a number of story plot ideas to consider by using mind-mapping techniques before drafting a written script. See *Sample Brainstorming for Story Plot Ideas* (p.118).

If you connect with your own mind deep enough, it reverberates for everyone. That's what we call art.

~ Natalie Goldberg

Telling someone about your experience breathes new life into it, moving it out of the inchoate swirl of unconsciousness into reality.

~ Mandy Aftel

Take Six: Elements of a Good Digital Story

There is a great deal to consider in constructing a digital story. While there are endless approaches to crafting stories depending on purpose and audience, at least six elements are considered fundamental to this particular storytelling style. The following six elements are woven into the narrative details of the seven digital storymaking steps.

1. Living Inside Your Story:

The perspective of each story is told as a personal experience with the content using your own voice to narrate the tale. You share throughout the story, what you feel and what this event or situation means for you in such a personal way that it engages viewers in a very real and emotional experience. Rather than a detached telling that this happened and that happened, viewers experience you living inside this story. The story is shared through the heart not the head.

2. Unfolding Lessons Learned:

One of the most unique features of this specific digital storytelling style is the expectation that each story express a personal meaning or insight about how a particular event or situation touched your own life. The development of this feature originated with Dana Atchley and Joe Lambert. A good story has a point to make, a moral conclusion, a lesson learned or an understanding gained. Each story needs to have a point that is revealed in the end either implicitly with the media or stated explicitly with words.

3. Developing Creative Tension:

A good story creates intrigue or tension around a situation that is posed at the beginning of the story and resolved at the end sometimes with an unexpected twist. There is a hook that draws the viewer into wondering how it will all end. Will the man get his fish? What does young girl find when she leaves home? Does Amber ever have friends? What is the meaning of having a life without a father? The tension of an unresolved situation engages and holds the viewer through the end. Pacing is an invisible part of sustaining story tension as we know so well from the era of Hitchcock films. Pacing uses starts, stops and pauses to make us wonder what is next and how the story will be resolved.

4. Economizing the Story Told: A good story has a destination – a point to make – and seeks the shortest path to its destination. Each digital story is no more than 3-5 minutes based on a script that is no more than one (1) page or 500 words. The art of shortening a story lies in preserving the essence of the tale — using the fewest words and images to make your point. By holding clarity about the essence of the story, the additional narrative that would normally be part of oral story-telling can be pared down.

5. Showing Not Telling: Good stories use vivid details to reveal feelings and information rather than just saying something was tall, happy, scary, or difficult to do. "It was a dark and stormy night" does not have to be said in the script. Unlike traditional oral or written stories, images, sound and music can be used to show a part of the context, create setting, give story information and provide emotional meaning not provided by words. Both words and media need to reveal through details rather than state the obvious.

6. Developing Craftsmanship: A good story incorporates technology in artful ways demonstrating exemplary craftsmanship in communicating with images, sound, voice, color, white space, animations, design, transitions, and special effects. All media elements are selected to extend the story meaning rather than engaging bells and whistles that become distracting, overused or misused. Good craftsmanship creatively combines media elements to convey significant meaning rather than "decorating" the story.

A Visual Map of Take Six: Elements

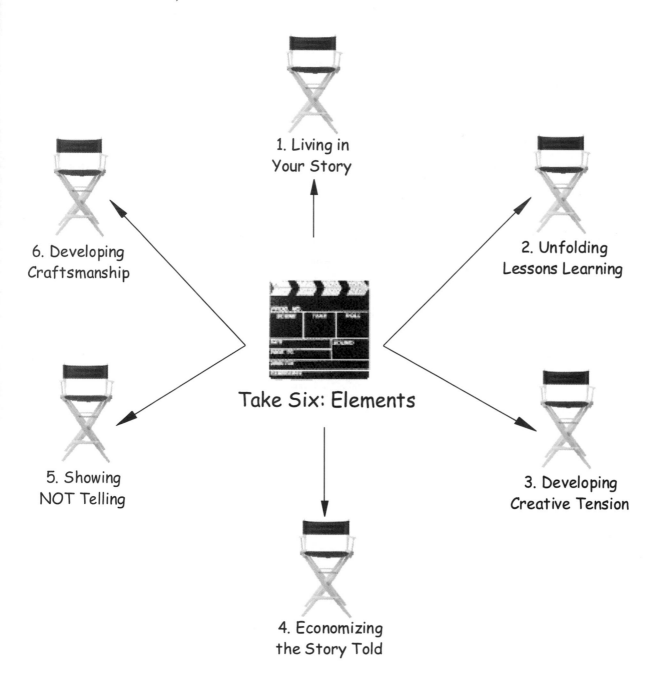

1. Living in
Your Story

6. Developing
Craftsmanship

2. Unfolding
Lessons Learning

Take Six: Elements

5. Showing
NOT Telling

3. Developing
Creative Tension

4. Economizing
the Story Told

Adapted from The Center for Digital Storytelling's Cookbook. Their work with essential story elements has inspired and informed my own work with digital storytelling. www.storycenter.org

Develop your story ideas by brainstorming story plots before organizing connections and arranging key ideas for the written script. Using *Inspiration* software may prove to be helpful to some writers in brainstorming, mind-mapping connections and arranging key ideas before drafting their first written script. (www.inspiration.com)

Regardless of how you develop the key ideas you want to express in your story, it is now time to write the script in sentence format. Just plunge in, remembering that you have time to revise, share out-loud and revise again until the script has the power and meaning you want it to have. You can't revise a blank page, so commit to starting with something, anything. Then give thanks for our word processing tools that make revising the story into a final copy a doable task!

TIP: Periodically try reading or telling your story out loud. Listen to the writing style. Does it represent the way you speak? Revise the sentence structure and vocabulary choices until the story has a conversational style that you might use with friends, family and colleagues.

The grace to be a beginner is always the best prayer for an artist. The beginner's humility and openness lead to exploration. Exploration leads to accomplishment. All of it begins at the beginning, with the first small and scary step.

~ Julia Cameron

Dancing Script Text and Media Together

As you write the script, stay aware that the story can be told with more than words. Multimedia tools now provide the storyteller with the artful ability to "show" ideas, feelings and events rather than being confined to simply "tell" their story with words. You are not limited to having to say with words "it was a dark and stormy night" in order to give the listener the story setting, mood or action. Ask how you can use images, sounds or music to create meaning, mood or understanding. The essential question to consider: is the written script filling in the meaning for the images and sound, or are the images and sound filling in the meaning of the text? Truthfully, text and media shape the story together. It is the script that defines the soul of the story, not the technical bells and whistles. Any way you approach this task, economizing the written lan-

The story is not in the plot but in the telling.

~ Ursula K. LeGuin

Sample Brainstorming of Story Plot Ideas

Here is a sample of brainstorming story plot ideas for my story called *Da Um Jeitinho*. This mind-map was created using Inspiration software. It is easy to use the "rapid fire" tool to generate a lot of ideas before organizing. Ideas are visually added, deleted and moved until they are finally shaped into your key story plot ideas.

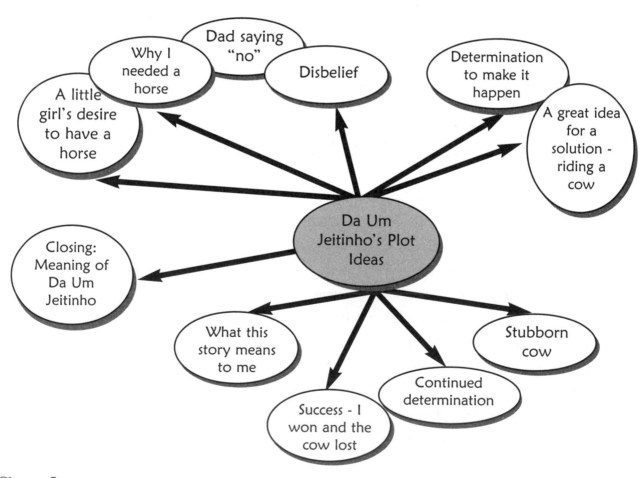

guage to incorporate varied media as a strong component in telling your story will be the greatest challenge in creating a script. You will be using a variety of media to accomplish what no single medium can do well alone.

Digital storytelling challenges us to consciously look for every possible way to edit out as many unnecessary words as possible before production. The purpose of shortening a story lies in preserving the essence of the tale — using the fewest words and images to make your point. By holding clarity about the essence of the story, the additional narrative that would normally be part of storytelling can be pared down by employing the media tools to tell a part of the context and meaning not provided by words. Even as you start your story idea with a script full of words, at the end of the digital production, text and media are ultimately combined to create a whole that is more than the sum of the parts.

Step 2. Planning the Project (Pre-Production Phase)

Remember the days of having to turn in an outline for your written essays and reports? I suspect that many of our schoolmates proceeded to do the report first and then created their outline afterwards to turn in because they didn't know what they were going to write until they did it. Digital stories have also been created without planning. However, the complexity of weaving all the media elements together into a cohesive story gives new meaning to planning FIRST! Digital storytellers will find it well worth the up front time to use these three general planning tools to prepare for production and post-production phases:

- Paper/electronic storyboarding
- Image/shot lists
- Music/sound lists

Tales are created from the world around us, given life by everything we know and understand, taken in through our senses, and gleaned from our memories. All we must do is pay close attention and when the image comes that promises a story, be willing to follow wherever it might lead.

~ Jimmy Neil Smith

Planning your digital story can save enormous amounts of time and energy. It will speed your digital project up in many useful ways. It eases frustrations of meeting deadlines or trying to wrap up a project. Professionals consider the storyboard an essential management and design tool. It is even more important for novice digital storytellers to use storyboards along with image/shot and music/sound lists to organize their voiceovers (scripts) with other media elements prior to production.

Planning Off-line Serves Four Purposes

1. Clarifying what media you need and do not need. You want to spend project time scanning, searching the Internet for resources, shooting video, editing photos, composing music or digitizing other media ONLY for what is needed by your story. Through planning, you can determine if you have too many or too few images or sounds. You can see where to trim or modify your script before you record.

2. Organizing the time sequence of the story to tell what happens first, next and last. It provides a pacing of all the media elements from beginning to end.

3. Detailing the interaction between voice, images, music, sounds, transitions, animations, and special effects. When shooting video, careful planning includes notations of angle, duration, panning and zooming for video elements. When mixing media, it ensures thoughtful choices.

4. Ensuring that the content of the story drives the uses of technology rather than getting diverted with "cool and fun" special effects.

TIP: Stories created by teams will need to give even more special attention and time to their planning steps in order to ensure quality, consistency and flow in their group stories. Group stories should not look like stitched quilts.

Developing Paper / Electronic Storyboards

Storyboards allow you to detail out all aspects of your story before you work on any of the media elements in the production and post-production stages. Storyboards come in all shapes and sizes, from using 4x6 cards to represent each scene or image frame to using basic paper graphic organizers. If the learning curves are not too steep, have some fun using electronic storyboarding templates and software. Storyboards may look similar to comic books but they are rarely polished. You are free to use rough sketches, keywords or symbols for the images that will be included in the story as you map out the scenes. For an electronic version of the sample storyboard in this chapter, see resources available at www.digitales.us under Story Making Files.

The length of a film should directly be related to the endurance of the human bladder.

~ Alfred Hitchcock

Featured Resource:
Atomic Learning's Electronic Story Boarding Software

Atomic Learning has created an electronic version of a storyboard. It is interesting, engaging and useful. However, learning to use the software will require time you may or may not want to spend at this point. It is, however, a resource worth investigating. (www.atomiclearning.com)

Sample Story Board Template

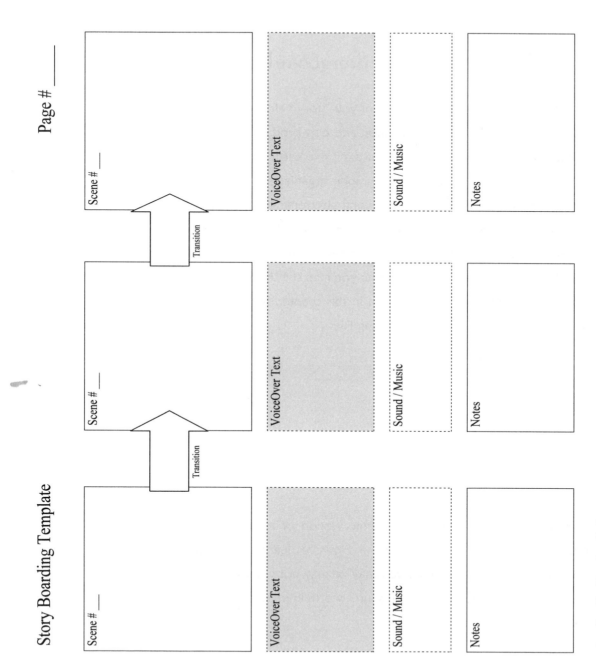

Story Boarding Template

Page # ____

Scene # ____   Transition   Scene # ____   Transition   Scene # ____

VoiceOver Text

Sound / Music

Notes

Developed by Bernajean Porter

Sequencing Elements in Storyboards

Start the Script. Place the script text that will later be a voiceover in your storyboard first. Be careful not to plan too many words for each frame. You don't want lines and lines under any single image frame. Expect the reading of each text line to take approximately six (6) to ten (10) seconds.

Plan Images. Rough out the flow of the text and images together before detailing the other elements. In general three (3) to four (4) seconds is the ideal length of time for each image to be displayed. If the image time is too short, it becomes hard for the viewer to connect with the picture. But if it is too long, viewers can get bored, restless and then begin to tune out. If you are not changing the image as frequently as suggested, plan some special effect to hold the viewer's interest. Sometimes special effects like panning or the use of the Ken Burns effect of creating movement such as zooming in on still images can hold a viewer's attention while lengthening the time the viewer sees a single image. Avoid long film footage clips of the same scene or dialogue. It is recommended to use no longer than 5-10 second video clips. You can stay on the same image subject but it is more interesting to cut to varied angles or views of your subject.

Add Titles. If the script text and images generally flow together well, titles can now be planned. The viewer is better served with large, limited key words. Choices of movement, color, font style and placement also create mood in the story.

Add Transitions. You may be able to sketch transitions in any time in the storyboard, but during the post-production phase, they are added after all the other visuals (images/titles) are finalized. In the actual post-production phase, transitions act like scotch tape that "sticks" to each side of both frames. This means transitions have to be deleted and re-entered in order to modify any image/title frames. Placing transitions after the script, images, and titles saves editing time.

Plan Music and Sound Effects. This element is generally the last to be added to your production. You may wish to jot down ideas but wait until the actual arranging of the other media in post-production before identifying the specific choices.

Add Notes ANYTIME. Jot down ideas, resources, memos, and other information that will help execute the storyboard when you move into production and post-production stages.

Every good story has mystery - not the puzzel kind, but the mystery of allurement.

~ Edudora Welty

Storyboards provide the "BIG" visual blueprint of all the detailed choices you make for each scene or image frame for your digital story before you begin production. Think of your storyboard as a work in progress that is modified as often as needed while keeping track of both the details and "big" picture of your story. As you begin to detail out your digital story, you will see what you have and what you need. You will want to create lists of needed images, video shots, music and sounds as you work on your storyboard. Further notations on the storyboard can be included to plan how the transitions, sounds, images, camera movement, special effects, voiceover and music will play out and fit together. Whatever storyboard approach you decide to use, the more details you can include, the more likely your project will flow during production time.

TIP: For sample storyboard templates and other planning resources, see Story Making Files under Resources at www.digitales.us.

Five Tips for Sequencing in Storyboards

Tip One: See guidelines for sequencing the elements in your storyboards. People often like it when projects and processes are broken down into steps. A messy process thus feels more manageable. While these are tips that have served many individuals and groups well, you are welcome to play renegade and do it your way. Storyboarding is in reality a recursive process since each element impacts and affects every other element.

Tip Two: If you are a teacher or leading a specific story development team, the storyboard is the place to "sign-off" on the quality of content and approach BEFORE students begin any production or post-production process-es. Coaching and making suggestions to improve the substance of the digital story is a lot easier here than making comments after all the technical work has been completed.

Tip Three: As you start to lay out the script and images together, you may discover that you need to pare the text down, change images, add images or take out a portion of the soundtrack to make it all work together. And that is the point of a detailed, thoughtful storyboard: better to have a map where you can move, change and modify the media elements until they work together the way you want them to. This is the place to do that mental work, and it is so much more efficient than relying on a trial and error approach in the post-production stage. Sequence the elements in your storyboard by starting with the script first, adding in images, titles, transitions and finally mixing in the music and sound elements last.

Tip Four: If the planning steps are skipped over, expect the time spent in post-production phase to increase considerably.

Tip Five: The same suggested sequence used to develop your storyboards will be used as the steps to mix the media elements together in the post-production process.

Pacing is Everything

One of the most invisible forces of good storytelling is the pacing of the story. Walk through your storyboard in your mind's eye. Imagine how it unfolds. This will help you be mindful of the pace you set as you detail out the various elements that will be used. Make notes of how the elements will be timed. Consider the pacing of your voiceover, how fast or slow you sequence images and special effects. Does the music or sound effects match the pacing needed to unfold the story? Fast pacing suggests urgency, action or danger. Slow pacing suggests reflection or savoring of a moment. Panning, for example, stretches our attention while a quick sequence of images stimulates our senses. Just as we might expect "white space" to be used for intentional effect in desktop publishing documents, digital stories also need breathing space to tell their tale. Leaving black empty space as the voice unfolds a piece of the story cre-

We want a story that starts out with an earthquake and works its way up to a climax.

~ Samuel Goldwyn

Sample Image / Shot List for Da Um Jeitinho Story

Image / Shot	Description	Source/
1. Title Page w/ cow image	Playful – maybe cartoonish - of three cows portraying the three title words	Internet search
2. Personal picture of little girl loving horses	Something that shows the charm of wanting a horse	Internet search
3. Pictures of real cow herds	Cows need to be pasturing IF possible – Full Shot	Internet search
4. Photo of me sitting on my horse as young child	Full shot – make object for overlay with cow herds	Scanned photo
5. Photo of cow pasture or cow lane with farm in the background	Need a wide shot for setting farm scene but with enough close-up (maybe panning) to show how rough it was to walk through	Internet search
6. Photo of black bull	Full shot – make object for overlay on cow pasture	Scanned photo
7. Black title screen saying NO	Large red 'NO' that pulses forward	Photoshop
8. Photo of me as little girl thinking of her imagined horse	Create an oval cut-out of head shot	Scanned school photo
9. Photo of "imagined horse"	Create feathered oval image	Internet search

ates dramatic attention. Silence or slow pacing techniques with voice, images or music draws the viewer into the experience to savor a moment or feel the intimacy being developed in the story. The art of pacing uses the starts, stops or pauses within the delivery to intentionally create tension and/or engagement in the story. Intentionally designing the story's pacing within the storyboard adds an important powerful quality to your story. Trust your own instincts for the rhythm that works best for your story.

Making Image or Shot Lists

After placing the text from your script into the storyboard, it is time to identify the images (still and video) needed to extend your story. Image/shot lists are just that — lists of what type of images and movie shots you want to accompany your story script. Gathering lots of images and film footage "just-in-case" you might need it can overwhelm you and your hard drive space. Storyboarding organizes more precisely the image resources you need.

In filmmaking the primary or sole media resource in the shot list is video film footage. However, in digital storytelling video clips, if used at all, are generally combined in small doses with other media like photos, artifacts, animations, graphics, drawings etc. Each video piece you choose for digital storytelling should be no longer than **5-15 seconds per clip**. Include descriptions in the image/shot list of the type of film shots, if any, you need to capture from existing footage or that you still need to shoot. Notes are made on the storyboard on whether you want to shoot wide shots (WS), full shots (FS), medium shots (MS), headshots (HS), close-ups (CU), or extreme close-ups (XCU).

The number of final images used will vary depending upon the length and style of your final product as well as how much video footage you choose to include. Use the images/shot lists to check off what you already have and what you still need. This may mean identifying photos or objects to scan, searching the Internet for specific images, or planning for additional photo shoots or film

Every time I get a script it's a matter of trying to know what I could do with it. I see colors, imagery.

~ Paul Newman

footage. No need to take time at this stage to edit images you expect to use. Still and scanned photos and original film footage can be cropped or edited later.

TIP: Using about 15-20 still images will give you about three to five minutes of digital story.

TIP: If you are working with a lot of video, it might be useful to view the specialized grammar of film productions.
(www.aber.ac.uk/media/Documents/short/gramtv.html)

TIP: Try reviewing some useful tips for creating a video that is presented in cartoon style can be found at Apple's site.
(www.apple.com/education/ilife/howto/imovie_tips)

TIP: For more technical details about images and video, see *Chapter 7: Entering the Technical World of Digital Media.*

Making Music or Sounds Lists

Like the images lists, it is also useful to plan a list of music and sounds needed after the initial storyboarding process has been completed. Music and sound effects have perhaps the most emotive power of any production element. They provide the tone, setting, mood and context for experiencing the text and images. Music can be used as dramatic introduction to establish setting, as background mood or tone, as non-verbal "showing" of meaning, or as a dramatic closing. Sounds add ambient reality as well as creating the setting. Giggles, clapping, barnyard animals, surf, a car door slamming, a phone ringing or lingering silence can draw your viewers into your story's meaning in dynamic ways. Music and sound provide so much emotional meaning that psome stories are quite literally created as tone poems using only sounds to tell the entire story.

Photography suits the temper of this age a perfect medium for active bodies and minds teeming with ideas.

~ Edward Weston

Sound is 50% of the motion picture experience.

~ George Lucas

Sample Music / Sound List for Da Um Jeitinho Story

Music / Sounds	Description	Source
1. Opening music that settles into background music for voiceover	Peppy, old fashioned, farmish tune	Composing in SmartSound: MovieMaestro software
2. Cow mooing	Must have cow displaying a stubborn attitude	Internet searching
3. Horse neighing	Frisky attitude	Internet searching
4. Ambient farm sounds for background	Chickens, pigs, donkeys, or tractors	Internet searching
5. Closing music for story ending	Child-like, willful, or determined lyrics	To be decided

While it is quite easy today to digitize or download any musical scores and songs, creating projects that will be shared in any way will need careful consideration of copyright laws. It is recommended you obtain written permission, subscribe to royalty free music libraries or consider investing in your own music production software to generate original music for your work.

TIP: Consider weaving guest voices into the written script to vary and deepen the story's emotional experience for listeners. Try inserting a grandmother's voice in her native language, a student's reaction to an experience, a father's musings on life, an expert's interview comments, or excerpts from a famous speech. Use them sparingly to ensure your own voice is telling YOUR story

TIP: You can find additional technical information and copyright friendly resources in *Chapter 6: Poof! Creating a DigiTales Toolkit* as well as *Chapter 7: Entering the Technical World of Digital Media.*

Step 3. Organizing Project Folders (Pre-Production Phase)

Each digital story is considered a project. Keep all sub-folders of resources and assets organized together with the final project. Many production tools reference the images, sounds, and other items from elsewhere on your hard drive rather than actually embedding the resources inside the software you are using to create your digital story. If these files are moved randomly or separately from the production file, then you will likely find yourself having to hunt down the location of the moved file and reconnect or "re-reference" it for the software program. The following seven (7) folders are recommended as a way of organizing your story files.

🗁 The "Project Folder" is considered the main folder (directory) that will contain all the other subfolders (subdirectories) of resources and assets related to this project. Make sure all files saved are directed to these folders. This folder can be housed on the desktop or within any of the hard drive document folders. Label this folder as *Project I*; *Bernajean's Project*; or *BJ's LifeStory Project* depending upon how private or public the storage area is for your project. You now need to create the following six (6) additional folders INSIDE the story's project folder. Do NOT move these folders or files out of the original project folder.

     📁   Images
     📁   ImagesEdited
     📁   MusicSounds
     📁   ProductionCopies
     📁   Script
     📁   VoiceOver

Step 4. Making the Voiceover (Production Phase)

Voiceovers are the digital files created by recording your final script in your own voice. While there may be digital stories told with only images and music, storytellers are encouraged to use their voices to provide personal content and meaning to their stories. Voice is the language of attitude that engages the audience in the emotion of the story. Find your voice and use it to establish a personal relationship with your listeners as the story is being told.

> Everything becomes a little different as soon as it is spoken out loud.
>
> ~ Hermann Hesse

Public speaking is often identified as one of the nation's most phobic experiences. Some people judge their own voices as less than perfect. Others feel stiff or self-conscious. But your voice with all its power and flaws expresses the real magic in your story because the story is told in a way that no other than you can deliver.

TIP: See *Chapter 6: Poof! Creating a DigiTales Toolkit* for specific optional hardware useful in creating very professional voiceover files.

TIP: For more technical details on creating a Voiceover, see *Chapter 7: Entering the World of Digital Media.*

Step 5. Gathering and Preparing Media Resources (Production Phase)

Now that your script has been drafted, performed and recorded, it is time to methodically gather and prepare the other media that you will weave together to extend the emotional power, depth and meaning of your story. This is a significant part of the production stage – producing the media elements you need to tell your digital story. The film industry calls the images, sounds and music that are used in movies "assets." Other groups call these media elements "resources."

You may or may not have already begun to gather these media files during the pre-production stage as you were scripting and/or storyboarding. The completed digitized voiceover does, however, provide the key organizer for the final selection of images, video shots, sounds, music and other elements used to unfold the story. Every story's media resources will be different. The technical tools and skills needed to complete this task provide a great playground for learning and making your story unique.

Using the image/shot lists along with the music/sound lists, decide which media will need to be gathered and prepared **prior** to the post-production stage. Many of the media elements may need editing, re-sizing or some type of customizing as part of the production process. A piece of music may need to be trimmed, a sound or "guest" voice normalized, a video clip cropped or graphic titles added into images. Some photo or scanned images may also need to be cropped, made into single objects for overlays or combined into a composite image. Composites can be as simple as a background with a single image having a text overlay. Or it can be a complex collage of images, graph-

Art is moral passion married to entertainment. Moral passion without entertainment is propaganda, and entertainment without moral passion is television.

~ Rita Mae Brown

ics or developing a specialized video-within-video composite scene. There are lots and lots of ways to engage your creativity.

TIP: Even though there are seven process steps outlined to guide you, digital storytelling as mentioned before is not a precise lock-step linear process. It is a creative process that takes its own path. Sometimes there are left turns — taking them may be the right intuitive thing to do. Other times a project deadline prohibits taking time for deviating from the storyboard in any significant ways. You decide.

TIP: For more technical details on gathering resources, see *Chapter 7: Entering the World of Digital Media.*

Keep it Simple First Time Around

Here is an important but gentle reminder for novices. Consider keeping technical demands and needs for storytelling simple in the beginning. Few people have the time, fortitude or natural talent to be a Steven Speilberg on their first project or two. For example, photo or video composites — mixing multiple stills or videos together — of any kind generally take multiple technical steps and possibly mastering more complex software like *PhotoShop*, *Final Cut* or *Premiere* that may have more functions but will also likely to have a higher learning curve as well. You might want to download an existing music track the first time or two rather than taking time to learn specialized software to compose your own soundtracks. This is where the time taken to develop a storyboard will pay off. Keep your storyboard close by in order to keep you focused on delivering the story rather than getting too lost in the technical playground. You will want to make sure a majority of your energy is spent on engaging your creativity in mixing the mediums to tell your tale. Again a major quality of a good story is to have soul first!

When Stories nestle in the body, soul comes forth.

~ Deena Metzger

TIP: Consider using an easy image-editing software product like Tech4Learning's *ImageBlender* to create interesting images without the cost and learning curves of more complex software programs. See *Chapter 6: Poof! Creating a DigiTales Toolkit.*

TIP: As you finish the digitizing, editing and preparation processes of your media resources, sort them into the project folder's subfolders (sub-directories), which you set up early on in Step Two.

TIP: You can find additional technical information for tips, ideas and resources in *Chapter 7: Entering the Technical World of Digital Media.*

Step 6. Putting it ALL Together (Post-Production Phase)

Do it BIG, do it right and do it with style.

~ Fred Astaire

You are now ready to spin your tale with digital tools. This is the post-production stage where all the elements are mixed together. Your ultimate goal is the viewer's total immersion in the story. You will want to draw the viewer into the story and keep them there as it unfolds. While your storyboard provides the initial decisions and elements, it is now time to follow your "gut" feeling regarding whether a particular way to move a story forward is the right one. Don't feel tied to using set formulas. The goal of the digital storyteller is to use the tools of the trade in such a way that the viewer sees and feels what the artist/director wants the audience to see or feel. It is great play space. Your storyboard should certainly guide you but NOT lock you in during this stage. If a brilliant, creative notion or approach strikes you in the middle of the production stage — go for it!

Mixing the Media

Add the media elements together in the following order for both the storyboarding planning and the sequence of mixing media with your video editing software tool:

1. Voiceover and guest voices
2. Images – stills, videos, animations, graphics, composites
3. Titles
4. Transitions
5. Music/sound effects

Gremlins Alert

Every digital story has its own technical challenges. Beware of technical "gremlins" that can creep into even the most experienced technology user's work. Creativity and interest can drain away fast when or if hardware or software functions start to break down or get in the way. For example, you do exactly what the manual tells you to do and it doesn't work. Or you do exactly what you did earlier but NOW it doesn't work. It should work – it did work – but it doesn't work. Go figure! Here are three strategies to save you some sanity:

1. Always, always save your work every five to ten minutes and especially after a section of editing has been completed. Use "save as" to make a back-up COPY with a new name intermittently – every three to four hours. The back-up copy is an important strategy that can save you from files that for no known reason become corrupt even though you JUST used them. If you are starting something new in your story that is a signal to save what you have now so you can come back to some known spot if things do get "gremlin-ed."

Any smoothly functioning technology will have the appearance of magic.

~ Arthur C. Clarke

If technology works, it is out of date.

~ Stafford Beer

2. Keep the magic of the project alive with adequate technical support on call. Sit next to someone who is more comfortable with technology. Bring a kid with you – they know how to do it even when they don't know how to do it. If you are leading a group in creating digital stories, you may want to consider providing one technical support staff for every five storytellers as a minimum safety net of support.

3. Practice saying out loud "oh well" while breathing or taking a brief walking break as you remember this is supposed to be fun! You can always go back to the last back-up copy you made – think back-up!

Make a Rough-Cut FIRST

There is a logical, time saving approach to mixing your media. It is useful to develop your digital story in two stages called rough-cut and final cut versions. First develop a "rough cut" digital version of the story without transitions, special effects and music/sound tracks. The rough-cut provides the author with a first view of the story sequence made up of just images and voiceover, titles screens, and "guest voices." The rough-cut review also saves the author some project time by determining what might still be missing or in need of additional editing. If you are going to revise the sequence or overall images, let it be at the rough-cut stage before all the other elements are mixed together.

Fine Tuning for The Final Cut

If the rough cut generally flows for you, begin fine-tuning the additional digital story elements. Titles, openings, closings, special effects, and transitions provide a world of playful creativity. Add music and sound effects LAST! If you modify any of the other elements, it changes the timing of the music's entry, exit and fades etc. However, this fine-tuning stage is also where novices can get overwhelmed or lovers of experimentation might find themselves bogged

Act as if what you do makes a difference...it does.

~ William Jones

down. Again, if the storyboarding step was skipped, it takes a lot more time to make all the post-production decisions.

Depending on project deadlines, storytellers may again want to consider keeping it simple the first time or two. If time is not a variable, enjoy playing with the field of choices and variations before wrapping up the project when you are ready. But beware the danger of eternal dabbling, polishing or modifying, thus creating a never-ending, never quite ever, ever finished story project!

TIP: Consider citing your sources with "rolling credits" at the story's end as well as adding any acknowledgements and other copyright references.

Step 7: Applause! Applause!

How shall I publish? Let me count the ways! What joy to finish a digital story! There is much to celebrate. When we share our stories, we experience a sacred time, a ritual that closes the story experience for individuals as well as groups who have been creating together. It is a time that celebrates the risks that each storyteller took in claiming a story worth telling. Everyone experiences pride, camaraderie, satisfaction and for many, enchantment with their work. The bringing together of a variety of media, combining them with the craftsmanship into a meaningful story – it is sheer delight for the soul.

In group workshops or home viewings, storytellers are often asked to give comments about their making-a-digital-story experience. After their digital story is shared with everyone, comments are invited from viewers based on their own experience with the story. However, this comment time should be structured very carefully — with respect and love. For further ideas and processes see Overview of Evaluation under Evaluating at www.digitales.us.

Anything less than reverence for each and every story can result in a deeply emotional sense of betrayal. People put themselves into these stories in ways that totally surprises them. Cherish every story.

~ Joe Lambert, Digital Storytelling

Publishing Formats

What playback or publishing format will you find most useful? Determine the preferred final output format by considering file sizes, bandwidth, media, and the resources available to your intended audience. Exporting to email or creating story files suitable for Web publishing is one great way to share with others. Exporting stories to DVD format is another popular way to distribute to friends, family, or colleagues for home or professional use. You can even port your movie to Bluetooth enabled cell phones to impress any and all friends or strangers.

Choose from the range of compression techniques (making the files smaller) and movie formats available in your video-editing software. Common choices include **MPEG** (Moving Picture Experts Group - cross platform but NOT editable after being put into this format), **AVI** (Audio-Video Interleave — a video format for Windows only) and **QT** or **MOV** (QuickTime — cross platform). QuickTime format choices range from full DVD quality, to Web, Web streaming or even email quality. QuickTime cross platform formats can also be imported into presentations or other multimedia software programs.

TIP: See more technical details in *Chapter 7, Entering the Technical World of Digital Media.*

TIP: File formats for the web are usually 240 x 180 ppi, which is often automatically calculated by the video-editing software when choosing Web quality compression.

TIP: Full DV quality expects a file format that is generally saved at 44.1 kHz at 16 bits, which is often automatically calculated by the video-editing software when choosing quality DV compression. The DV quality is affected by the speed and frequency of how often the information is sampled. The more often and faster it is sampled, the higher quality and the larger the memory needed. For medium DV quality you want no less than 22 kHz and not less than 8 bits.

TIP: Whichever format(s) you decide to use, be sure to create a back up of all the project folders with original resources. Carefully cite all sources, saving any permission given to use copyright materials used in your project.

In Conclusion

And now each digital story lives happily ever after . . . literally a living artifact that each storyteller now leaves as a personal legacy to others.

Tell your tales; make them true. If they endure, so will you.

~ James Keller

Chapter 6

Poof! Creating a DigiTales Toolkit

If a man smiles all the time he's probably selling something that doesn't work.

~ George Carlin, Brain Droppings

Let's Go Shopping!

Digital media comprises a world of technical tools, skills and terminology. Movie making is a skill that people often spend years mastering with very expensive equipment in specialized schools. Just as there are a few people who write for a living and many others who use word processing for personal projects, so the complex media tools used by many professionals in their fields have now become easy, inexpensive, and full-of-fun tools for the rest of us.

So now that we can all do it, where do you start? What hardware do we need? What software? The shopping choices can be overwhelming for most beginners who are ready to plunge into digital storytelling but are not sure where to start. While beginners will get basic start-up information here on putting their **DigiTales Toolkit** together, this chapter is not meant to eliminate other choices of specific software and hardware. Because the choice of tools in the marketplace will likely change over time, it is possible that the specific technologies in this section will become out-of-date or superceded by even better choices. However, generic details and information about the best-of-the-best resources today are provided here to enable non-experts to get a handle on the technology choices needed to get their digital stories (movies) started. Visit my Website for ongoing updates. (www.digitales.us)

Everything that I've learned about computers at MIT I have boiled down into three principles: Unix: You think it won't work, but if you find the right wizard, he can make it work. Macintosh: You think it won't work, but it will. PC/Windows: You think it won't work, and it won't.

~ Philip Greenspun

In the Beginning ... You Need a Computer

Today's personal computers put more speed, more memory and more capacity than ever at our fingertips. But powerful hardware is only a foundation. Software is what turns that box of wires and chips into a digital movie studio. While digital storytelling can be created with all hardware platforms, it must be said that several aspects of Macintosh's hardware and software ease the learning curves and processes, making it ideally suited to digital media work. Basic digital media software called *iLife* now comes installed at no charge with all Macintosh workstations while PC Windows users will need to add this type of software and add a few hardware components at some additional cost. Because the *iLife* programs (*iTunes, iPhoto, iMovie, iDVD* and most recently the *Garage Band* for music composition) are integrated, their functions and files work smoothly together with the hardware. Combining media is easy, simplified and reliable because *iLife* programs were designed to work together. (www.apple.com/ilife/video/)

Equivalent digital video production programs are available and identified in this chapter for PC's running Microsoft Windows. But the suite of tools and hardware components needed for digital video production are generally not included with every Windows PC. Therefore, PC owners not only need to identify a number of vendor products and hardware add-ons on their own, but also spend more dollars as well as be good consumers to deal with a myriad of technical compatibility issues so that their media programs work together.

The *iLife* software automatically performs technical conversions behind the scenes, such as translating the 4X3 aspect ratio of **720x534 pixels** images into squashed **640x480 pixels** suitable for DVD and TV formats. The technical image conversion between computer screen and TV formatting at this time is an added step needed when using varied PC Windows software. Mac's *iLife* streamlines the exporting and importing as well as transporting file formats between tools. Media on the Mac can be transported from inside each *iLife* program with a simple click. You can also simply "drag and drop" media files between programs. For example a music track from *iTunes* can be "dragged" directly into the windows of *iPhoto, iMovie*, or the *iDVD* tools.

It is highly recommended that anyone wanting to purchase a personal computer for digital media production projects that will be more fun than effort consider investing in a ready-to-go Macintosh computer. But if a Windows PC is your machine of choice, digital storytelling software tools are also identified to help consumers get started.

I think there is a world market for maybe five computers.

~ Thomas J. Watson

Getting Ready Checklist

Do you have the tools necessary for pre-production, production, post-production and distribution work? Before launching a project, check out the readiness of your hardware, software tools, and file management capacity.

Hardware Readiness

☐ Workstation: memory, speed, and internal hard drive space

☐ Digital cameras: still and movie

☐ Digitizing capacity: images, sound and voice

☐ Internet capacity: access and bandwidth

☐ Scanner

☐ Printer

☐ CD and DVD burner(s)

☐ Multi-media headsets

Software Readiness

☐ Pre-production writing and storyboarding tools

☐ Production image capturing/editing tools

☐ Production sound capturing/editing tools

☐ Production music composition tools

☐ Post-production mixing and editing media tools

☐ Distribution file format(s)

File Management Readiness: Storage and Transfer

☐ Network or external hard drives for file sharing and/or transferring

☐ Storage area(s) for project files

☐ Back-up area(s) or mediums for project files

Functions, Functions, Functions

Regardless of which platform you choose to develop your digital stories, shopping for the right hardware and software is still a big job even for techno savvy users. There are SO-O-O many variables that it is easy to get lost or be vendor vulnerable in the land of consumerism. Some vendors claim functions and you discover it is possible but more difficult or more steps than it is worth to make something work. For example, as we were choosing voice recording software, all of them seem to do the job. Some were cheaper than others. But our final choice was based on having as few steps as possible, the necessary functions, AND also being more intuitive than the others at getting the voice recording job done. Some products may seem the same but they either fall short or have a lot more functions than you will need. It is reasonable to want what you need but not to pay for any more than will do the job.

To help you in jump-starting your shopping spree for a **DigiTales Toolkit**, skim these chapter sections.

- **DigiTales Software Toolkits**
- **Software Descriptions**
- **Hardware Function Checklists**
- **Software Seven Step Process Function Checklists**

DigiTales Software Toolkits

This section identifies a software toolkit to consider for both PC and Mac platforms. Whenever possible software programs that are available for both platforms were chosen over software developed for only one platform. There may be other programs out there that suit your needs better or become available after this book is printed. These **DigiTales Toolkits** recommendations are meant to give beginners a starting place in the market place.

Retail costs are listed to give a sense of the expense involved but prices may change or be available at discounts. Be sure to shop around for education or academic pricing (academicsuperstore.com) if you qualify. Many catalogue and online discount stores also have specials for the general public that can make the overall retail cost much lower.

Some software tools are considered essential or BASIC. Generally the software tools that are identified as BASIC have streamlined features making them easier to learn and less expensive. The BASIC tools will be plenty for amateur hobbyists who are not likely to need the high-end functions or be inclined to invest more learning time and dime to have more features.

Other software tools are identified as advanced or PRO. Generally the software tools that are identified as PRO have more functions, longer learning curves and can cost more. The PRO tools will generally be more suited to professionals, serious hobbyists, or long-term specific classes whose needs for more features are going to be worth the investment of more time and dimes.

If you are working with younger children, ideally we want them to use technology tools that can easily be mastered so the majority of their attention and brain energy can be on their ideas and work rather than learning the tool. Yes, some older kids and adults also like starting with streamlined tools as well. These kid-friendly tools are likely to have features such as colorful interfaces, simple menus, and intuitive icons. Imaging editing tools like Tech4Learning's *ImageBlender* is a good example of these kind of features plus ease of use. On the other hand, young tech-savvy storytellers are very capable of using the BASIC Tools listed for MACS and WINS platforms. Don't underestimate them! See **DigiTales Toolkits** at www.digitales.us for suggested updated software products, vendor information and special recommendations for kids.

If you are just getting started, not expecting to do professional work, wanting ease-of-use, or working with a tight budget then the BASIC programs will give

This 'telephone' has too many shortcomings to be seriously considered as a means of communication. The device is inherently of no value to us.

~ Western Union internal memo, 1876.

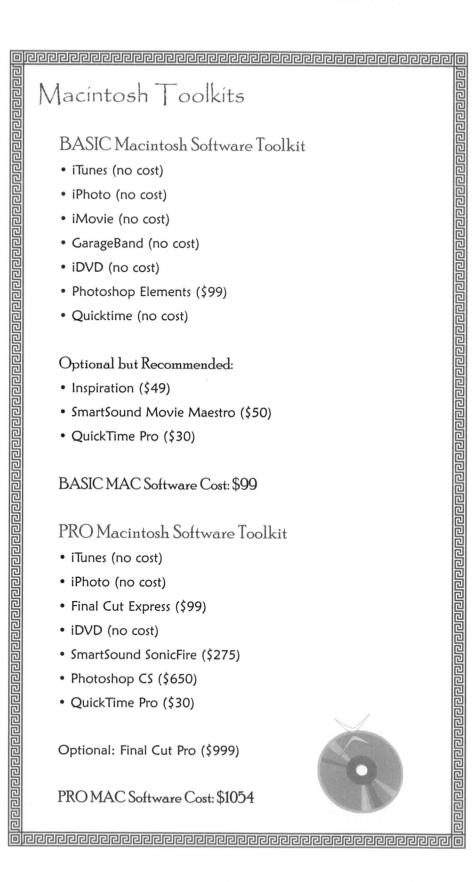

Macintosh Toolkits

BASIC Macintosh Software Toolkit

- iTunes (no cost)
- iPhoto (no cost)
- iMovie (no cost)
- GarageBand (no cost)
- iDVD (no cost)
- Photoshop Elements ($99)
- Quicktime (no cost)

Optional but Recommended:

- Inspiration ($49)
- SmartSound Movie Maestro ($50)
- QuickTime Pro ($30)

BASIC MAC Software Cost: $99

PRO Macintosh Software Toolkit

- iTunes (no cost)
- iPhoto (no cost)
- Final Cut Express ($99)
- iDVD (no cost)
- SmartSound SonicFire ($275)
- Photoshop CS ($650)
- QuickTime Pro ($30)

Optional: Final Cut Pro ($999)

PRO MAC Software Cost: $1054

PC Windows Toolkits

BASIC PC Windows Software Toolkit

- iTunes (no cost)
- Uleads' VideoStudio 8 ($99)
- Photoshop Elements ($99)
- QuickTime (no cost)

Optional but Recommended:
- Inspiration ($49)
- SmartSound Movie Maestro ($50)
- QuickTime Pro ($30)

BASIC WIN Software Cost: $198

PRO PC Windows Software Toolkit

- iTunes (no cost)
- Adobe Premiere Express ($99)
- SmartSound Sonic Fire ($275)
- Photoshop CS ($650)
- QuickTime Pro ($30)

Optional: Adobe Premier Pro ($700)

PRO WIN Software Cost: $1054

If computers get too powerful, we can organize them into a committee -- that will do them in.

~ Bradley's Bromide.

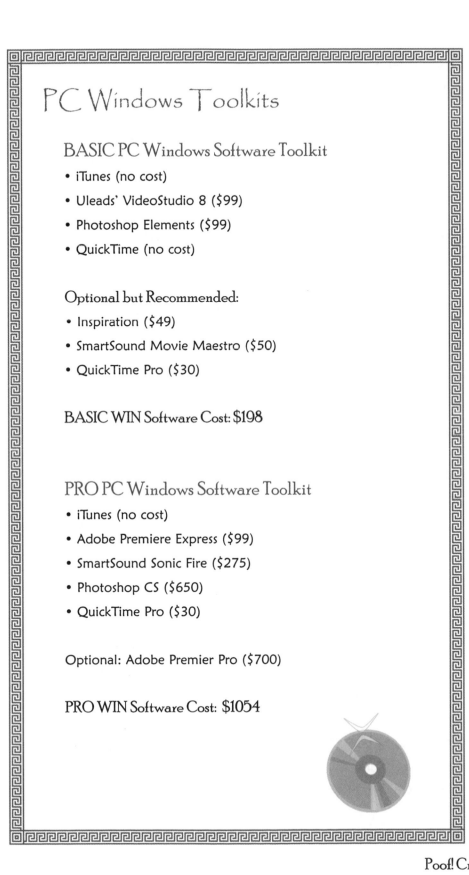

Free Software Downloads

- **Blue Armadillo** (MAC and WIN) is a free image batch conversion utility. Use this software to convert an entire folder of images from one format to another, one size to another, add a uniform effect to all of the images, or any combination of these. Blue Armadillo requires Macintosh System 8.1 or higher, or Windows 95 or higher. (www.tech4learning.com/snacks/barmadillo.html)

- **Gee Three Slick Transition Samplers** (MAC) This vendor provides a small sampler from their multitude of additional transitions for iMovie. (www.geethree.com/)

- **iTunes** (MAC and WIN) Manages music and sound files. Most useful to export files in various formats. www.apple.com/itunes/download/

- **Morpheus Software** (WIN) Morphing is the process of transforming one image into another. (www.morpheussoftware.net/)

- **QuickTime** (MAC and WIN) This is a free player that handles popular audio, video and graphic formats such as MPEG, 3GPP, Flash, AVI, AIFF, JPEG, GIF, WAV, MPEG-4 and AAC. (www.download.com)

- **Photoshop Album Starter Edition** (WIN) This is a free photo management program from Adobe. It features a few of the features that come with the regular Album program frequently bundled with *Photoshop Elements* in order to manage photographs. (www.adobe.com/products/photoshopalbum/starter.htm)

- **Windows Movie Maker 2** (WIN) Makes great slideshows of stills and videos into movies. This program has a number of features but one major digital storytelling limitation. It only has a single audio track for composition. You can either have voice narration or sounds or music but only one at a time, not the combination of narration PLUS music/sound considered necessary to unfold personal digital stories. Movies that are created can only be saved and viewed with Windows Media Player. Rather than having files that can be viewed by everyone – viewers are required to own a Windows machine. Cross platform formats are preferred: AVI and QuickTime. (www.microsoft.com/windowsxp/moviemaker/downloads/moviemaker2.asp)

you plenty of features and plenty of quality. Feel free to mix and match the BASIC tools with some of the PRO software tools if you want.

Software Descriptions

General descriptions of each software program are provided to understand the overall purpose of each tool. These descriptions will also give you an idea of what to look for if you decide to shop for tools other than those identified in the DigiTales Toolkits. It is essential when shopping to do extra checking that the software will run with your present hardware configurations. Be sure to check out vendor Websites for further descriptions and view their movie tutorials featuring their products. They will give you an overview of the key features and "selling points." Some Websites offer product comparisons and user reviews to browse. It might also be useful to view and compare general features using MAC and WIN free software tutorials at www.atomiclearning.com.

Computing is not about computing anymore. It is about living.

~ Nicholas Negroponte

Pre-production Software Tools

Inspiration (MAC and WIN) is a visual and thinking tool. It incorporates graphical icons and mind-mapping features to use while brainstorming ideas, clarifying thinking, and to process, organize and prioritize new information. It also stimulates creative thinking by allowing you to combine, delete, add and modify relationships between and among ideas. This tool is especially helpful during the script writing stage for generating, arranging and expanding on story plot ideas. Free trial versions available. (www.inspiration.com)

I'm all in favor of keeping dangerous weapons out of the hands of fools. Let's start with typewriters.

~ Frank Lloyd Wright

Atomic Learning's Electronic Storyboarding (MAC and WIN) provides an online organizer for planning images, sound and transition elements. (www.atomiclearning.com)

Production Software Tools

GarageBand (MAC) is the newest member of the *iLife* series. Create, record and perform your own original copyright free music complete with pre-recorded loops, amps, effects, and editing tools. *GarageBand* has over 1000 musical loops created with more than 30 instruments. Users drag-and-drop these loops — drum loops, bass loops, piano loops — into a timeline, layering the loops into original compositions. Or you can record into the timeline with your own midi keyboard, guitar or microphone attached to your computer. While it does take some musical appreciation and creativity, *GarageBand* is a great solution to having copyright friendly musical scores to enhance movies and slideshows. (www.apple.com/ilife/garageband)

iTunes (MAC and WIN) is considered a digital music jukebox. *iTunes* supports a variety of music formats including MP3 along with the new AAC – a new cutting-edge audio code. *iTunes* is now available free for both platforms. If you are using the *iLife* series for the Macintosh, every *iTune* song can be used with *iPhoto, iMovie and iDVD*. Your music is never more than a mouse click away when you're creating a slideshow in *iPhoto*, adding an audio track to a movie you're producing in *iMovie* or looking for the perfect song for a motion menu in *iDVD*. Free downloads are available. (www.apple.com/itunes/download)

iPhoto (MAC) organizes digital photographs. It is an all-in-one application for importing, organizing, editing and sharing your digital photos. Importing from cameras, CDs or simply dragging a folder of images from your desktop into the album area of *iPhoto* is a simple one-click process. Photos can be sorted, enhanced (brightness/contrast), resized, and cropped. An essential feature for movie-making is the automatic resizing and "squashing" of photos in order to be ready for the pixel ratio change needed for TV viewing. Before this *iPhoto* feature, all photos first had to be imported into special software like *Photoshop*. Then the photo had to be resized from 720x534 pixels to 640x480 in order to be used. *iPhoto* makes this process seamless by automat-

If it's green, it's biology, If it stinks, it's chemistry, If it has numbers it's math, If it doesn't work, it's technology.

~ Unknown

All technology should be assumed guilty until proven innocent.

~ David Brower

ically getting the image sized for TV viewing when importing into *iMovie* or *iDVD. iPhoto's* translation feature saves a lot of technical steps and file management. (www.apple.com/education/ilife/howto)

ImageBlender (MAC and WIN) A very, very user-friendly image editing tool with lots of features to customize images. This software has more features than *iPhoto* or *Photoshop Album* with a lot more ease than using *Photoshop Elements.* You can blend more than one image, make letter or image shapes, paint and draw, add text, and enjoy experimenting with many special filter effects. After preparing images, users can also make electronic storybooks (images, transitions plus voice narration) or photo essay slide shows. Download a free thirty-day fully functioning trial version. Online tutorials available. (www.Tech4Learning.com)

PhotoShop Album (WIN) organizes digital photographs. Photographs can be imported from cameras, CDs, scanners or computer. You can even import video and audio. Painting effects are available, along with photo restoration, color correction and the ability to create seamless panoramas. Text labels with 3D effects, drop shadows and even text warping can be applied to the photo. Photographs are easily imported into *Photoshop Elements* for more advance editing features including being able to crop and resize (720x480) the photos for TV viewing. Free Starter Edition available. (www.adobe.com)

Photoshop Elements (MAC and WIN) has as many image editing tools as most people who are not professional will need. Selection tools are highly precise; color correction and adjustments along with its layering ability making *PS Elements* a program for serious hobbyists. You can adjust shape, size, orientation, contrast, and color in images, and create animations, layers and panoramas. Or you can add text and other objects to images for composites of all kinds. These features provide high-powered editing not found in iPhoto and Photoshop Album. The package comes at a great price for the features provided. The learning curve is very doable if you want to do more than minor editing. (www.adobe.com/products/photoshopel/main.html)

Where a new invention promises to be useful, it ought to be tried.

~ Thomas Jefferson

Photoshop CS (MAC and WIN) provides more features at a higher price. High-end imaging modes, such as CMYK are essential for print-oriented professionals. Automated workflows through the Actions palette, integration with ImageReady (Web supported designing), Channels and Paths palettes, Dynamic Level tracking, and use of 95 special effects filters are examples of *CS's* sophisticated editing tools. Serious photo or image hobbyists or professionals will enjoy this program. (www.adobe.com/products/photoshop/overview.html)

QuickTime (MAC and WIN) is a free player version that plays many kinds of file formats, including video, audio, graphics, and virtual reality (VR) movies. Editing features do not come with this no-cost version. (www.apple.com/quicktime)

QuickTime Pro (MAC and WIN) is a very cost effective video editing program. *QuickTime Pro* is first a great low cost tool for converting one type of file format to anther. It imports multiple standard image, video or sound file format into over a hundred other standard file formats. It imports jpeg, AVI, MPEG 1-4, animated GIFs, Flash, MP3, WAV, *QuickTime* and DV formats. *QuickTime* then exports to numerous formats including AVI, MPEG-4, WAVE, QuickTime, BMP, AIFF or into DV Internet Streaming. *Quicktime Pro* also provides a few editing features that enable some advance editing features not found in the low end video editing tools. (*iMovie, MovieMaker*) You are able to extract, edit and manipulate multiple tracks of video and audio. QuickTime assigns layer numbers to each video and sound track added. These layers can be individually edited before recombining into a single movie. This is a powerful tool for creating cool special video effects like masking, mattes, transparency, and videos within videos. Movies can easily be combined with other movies, pictures or sounds. They can also be sized with various audio choices. You can purchase a registration key to upgrade from the free version of *QuickTime* to *QuickTime Pro.* (www.apple.com/quicktime/buy/)

SmartSound Movie Maestro (MAC and WIN) is the friendliest and easiest copyright free music-making program available that still gives you control over the creative process. It offers two approaches to creating soundtracks for your movies. First, you can import a movie and then place multiple songs, edit and manipulate the music in real-time to score it. Second, you can create songs without an imported movie using fully orchestrated soundtracks. Unlike the many loop creation programs that require editing individual tones and layering multiple instruments and sounds in a project file, *SmartSound* offers an intuitive, easy-to-use interface combined with studio-produced music. No time consuming sound editing or music composition is needed. Your customized soundtracks can be exported in a variety of file formats to use in other programs. It is packaged with 26 selections with optional data disks for purchase. (www.smartsound.com)

SmartSound SonicFire (MAC and WIN) has the ease of using soundtracks found in the Movie Maestro software with many more features and editing tools. Edit with precision any sound file including audio CD's. *SonicFire* uses advanced tools like *Razor*, *SmartExtend* and block controls. Search, audition and purchase additional soundtracks in real time from a vast SmartSound library via the InterNet. *Sonicfire Pro* now integrates with *Avid*, *Final Cut Pro and Express*, *Premiere Pro*, *Flash MX*, *PowerPoint*, *Video Studio 8*, *iMovie*, and many more. The program supports Windows Media and Quicktime file formats. It is packaged with 42 library selections with an optional feature to search, preview and download online for a song-by-song purchase from SmartSound Library. (www.smartsound.com)

Post-Production Software Tools

Adobe Premiere Elements (WIN) is not only significantly lower in cost than Adobe Premiere Pro but also simplifies and automates many of the more complicated functions found in Pro. Many "How-To's" tutorials are built in to view as you step through the editing process, from transferring footage to burning

The art of our era is not art, but technology. Today Rembrandt is painting automobiles; Shakespeare is writing research reports; Michelangelo is designing more efficient bank lobbies.

~ Howard Sparks

DVDs. There are hundreds of professional-quality special effects. This post-production tool is for the serious hobbyist but not ready for high-end professional PRO video editing.

Adobe Premiere Pro (WIN) is a popular choice of video editing programs among the industry professionals. It features nonlinear real-time precise management of every aspect of your video projects. The interface is quite complex so some media experience or support is recommended. It does, however, help that familiar Adobe standard tools and short cuts are used. *Premiere Pro* offers a huge variety of options and editing tools. The 99+ video and audio tracks provide for endless compositions. The program provides a tight integration with *Adobe After Effects*, *Adobe Photoshop CS* and *Adobe Encore DVD*. It supports a plug-in — *SmartSound Quicktracks* ($99) — that lets you search, audition, purchase and download from the entire *SmartSound* library of royalty free music right into your *Adobe Premiere* project file. This program has extensive import and export formats.
(www.adobe.com/products/premiere/overview.html)

iMovie (MAC) is part of *iLife's* software package. It is a post-production tool. It provides easy video capture and basic editing capabilities for those new to media manipulation. iMovie has two (2) audio and one (1) video tracks, considered the bottom-line number of tracks needed for storytelling. This enables music/sound and voice narration to play simultaneously. Any video composites needing more than one video track — video on video or still images on video — can be done with *iMovie's* special effects or *QuickTime Pro*. You can easily add photos directly from *iPhoto* libraries and songs from *iTune* libraries with just a click. Multiple file formats of images, videos or sound files on the desktop can be dragged and dropped directly into the timeline without converting or importing. Trim video and sound clips, extract the sound from video, sync video and sound tracks, and control the sound level of sound tracks with ease. Titles, transitions, special effects (including the Ken Burns image motion effect) can be customized and inserted with a simple click. Movies can be shared directly from the program onto the Internet, sent to

If the automobile had followed the same development as the computer, a Rolls-Royce would today cost $100, get a million miles per gallon, and explode once a year killing everyone inside.

~ Robert Cringely

friends in emails, made into a *QuickTime* movie for a variety of presentations or taken with you on Bluetooth devices. *iMovie* and *iDVD* work together seamlessly making the creation of DVDs easy. Click the *iDVD* button within *iMovie* and set your chapter marks. Then click "Create an *iDVD* project" to export your film directly into *iDVD* where it can be dressed up with Hollywood-style features: customized motion themes, soundtracks, interactive menus and special effects. (www.apple.com/education/ilife/howto)

Final Cut Express (MAC) is a more up scale video editor having robust and innovative editing, effects, and compositing features. It is not only lower in cost than *Final Cut Pro* but simplifies many of the more complicated options of *Pro*. It has real-time compositing, color correction and special effect tools. There are 99 video compositing layers to recreate animations, motion paths, time effects and frame blending. It also has up to 99 tracks of audio (eight in real time) to mix and match voice, sound effects and music. You can edit and enhance audio with transitions and filters. There is also support inside the program to record a high quality VoiceOver. This tool is for the serious but not ready for professional video editor. *Final Cut Express* works in perfect harmony with all *iLife* programs. (www.apple.com/finalcutexpress)

Final Cut Pro (MAC) is a popular choice of video editing programs among industry professionals and includes features similar to AVID Express. The interface is quite complex, so some media experience or support is recommended. The program includes over 150 real-time-capable effects, transitions, and filters. It can play back or preview high-quality simultaneous streams and effects. You work in 1080i and 720 HD (high definition) from start to finish without managing multiple offline formats. You can capture DV, SD and HD video formats over firewire and output to a wide range of formats. You can also create custom soundtracks and audio with the embedded Apple's *SoundTrack* tool for music composition. Think of it as a jazzed up *iLife's GarageBand*. The program lets you import and export *iMovies* as well as export to *iDVD* with chapter marks. (www.apple.com/finalcutpro)

The telephone has too many short comings to seriously be considered as a means of communication.

~ Western Union, 1876

MediaBlender (MAC and WIN): A easy tool for hyper-interactive stories using text, sound, graphics, movies, images and navigation tools that will create twist-a-plots and choose-your-own adventures. If you have used *Hyperstudio*, this software is a seamless transition that also imports existing *Hyperstudio* projects. Web-ready projects make distributing stories for others easy. Download a free fully functioning trial version. (www.Tech4Learning.com)

Ulead's VideoStudio 8 (WIN) gives you every tool you need to easily capture video to your computer, edit it, add titles, music, narration and special effects. It has two (2) video tracks and (2) audio tracks to mix and match still images, videos, titles, transitions, and special effects. *VideoStudio 8* allows for robust video editing with easy to use features: frame-by-frame editing, adding titles, 3D transitions, animations, video composites, scene transitions, fast/slow motion effects, surround sound mixer, noise reduction and DVD menus. Integrates seamlessly with *SmartSound* music files. Movies export into a number of file formats for viewing on both platforms. This software comes with great DVD tutorials and video production guides.
(www.ulead.com/vs/features.htm)

Distribution Software Tools

iDVD (MAC) is a part of the *iLife* series. It integrates seamlessly with *iPhoto*, *iMovie*, *GarageBand*, and *iTunes*, allowing access to all your individual images, movies (with chapter marks) and songs through a built-in media browser. Everything can be imported directly or "dragged and dropped" from program to program as well as directly using files on the desktop. Customize presentation themes, text on the screen, interactive buttons, transitions, sound-tracks and other special effects create a Hollywood style DVD for family and friends. (www.apple.com/ilife/idvd/)

There is no reason anyone would want a computer in their home.

~ Ken Olson, President of Digital Corps, 1977.

Workstation Function Checklist

- ❑ Memory – more is better! Minimum 512 MB RAM and 60 Gig harddrive. Recommended 1 Gig RAM and 80-120 Gig harddrive.
- ❑ Processor speed – faster is better! Minimum 600 Mhz.
- ❑ Fire wire cards for importing and exporting files standard in all new MACS. PC WINDOWS will need to add a Firewire PCI card — be sure you have an empty slot and and know that the card will not interfere with existing device drivers. Some WIN computers are now including this as an option.
- ❑ Sound cards – Standard on all MACS. Some WIN computers are now including this as an option.
- ❑ CD burners – Standard on most computer configurations
- ❑ DVD burners

  MACS need to add the SuperDrive option in order to burn disks using *iDVD* – external DVD burners will NOT work with *iDVD*. PC WINS need to add this option.

Specialized Hardware Function Checklist

- ❑ Internet connection – high speed and wireless would be useful!
- ❑ Multi-media headphone OR external microphone
- ❑ An analogue to digital video converter box
- ❑ A color flatbed scanning station
- ❑ An external fire wire 200+ gig hard drive
- ❑ A digital movie camera w/ tripod and fire wire connection
- ❑ A still digital camera with USB connection
- ❑ Optional: A PRO Voiceover Recording Station (p.172)

Hardware Function Checklists

What you buy depends on identifying what you want to do. As soon as this book goes to press, new products will surely be developed the day after. By reviewing these checklists, you can do comparison shop with other products not mentioned in this chapter.

Software Seven Step Process Function Checklists

This checklist organizes the functions for digital storytelling software tools using the four phases for making a digital story: Pre-production, Production, Post-Production, and Distribution. There are seven process steps within these phases that need different tools at different times. Software is listed for BASIC functions within each of the seven processing steps for making digital stories along with a few notes identifying PRO software when useful.

TIP: The PRO video editing programs (*Final Cut* and *Adobe Premiere*) do have voiceover capturing tools and some limited editing functions as part of their program features. You may still want to invest in external multi-media head-phones or external microphones to increase voice capturing quality with these video-editing software programs.

TIP: If you do a lot of recording or work with an on-going class or group, high-end audio capturing software will serve you well as the normalizing feature which is not in the PRO video-editing software listed here. Normalizing is the process of increasing overall volume of an audio recording to maximum volume without distorting. This creates a very robust voice presence.

TIP: However you choose to digitize voices, test and ensure you have crisp and clear voice narratives without background or white noise.

Everything that can be invented has been invented.

~ Charles Duell, Commissioner of US Patent Office 1891 proposal to close down.

Pre-Production Phase: Planning the Story	Pre-Production Functions	BASIC Software Tools Used
1. Writing a Script	❏ Brainstorming ❏ Mind Mapping ❏ Writing	• Word processor • *Inspiration*
2. Planning the Project (story-boarding, image/shot lists, music/sound lists)	❏ Templates ❏ Graphic Organizers ❏ Electronic Storyboarding	• Word processor • *Inspiration* • *Atomic* Electronic Storyboards
3. Organizing Project Folders on the Desktop for Resources	N/A	N/A

Production Phase: Gathering and Preparing Media Resources	Production Functions	BASIC Software Tools Used
4. Making the VoiceOver	❏ Audio Capturing ❏ Equalizing – this increases and decreases the level of certain frequencies – PRO only ❏ Normalizing – increases overall volume of an audio recording to maximum volume with distorting creating a very robust voice presence – PRO only	• Built-in computer audio capture recording used by *iMovie, Final Cut, VideoStudio 8* or *Premiere* • Equalizing with *iMovie, Final Cut, VideoStudio 8* or *Premiere* • Normalizing – (PRO only) this feature will need to use the Pro-Recording Station software: *Bias Peak 4 LE* Recording (MAC) or *Sound Forge* (WIN)

Production Phase: Gathering and Preparing Media Resources cont'd	Production Functions	BASIC Software Tools Used
5. Gathering Image Media Resources	❑ Filming / using digital video images ❑ Analog to Digital Video conversion ❑ Using still camera images ❑ Using photo CD images ❑ Scanning photos, objects, memorabilia ❑ Creating own graphics or artwork ❑ Finding online downloads	• *iPhoto* • *Photoshop Album* • Scanning into *Photoshop* • Internet Browser
5. Gathering Music/Sound Resources	❑ Digitizing CD music/sound effects ❑ Creating own music/sound effects Finding online downloads	• *iTunes* • *SmartSound Movie Maestro* • *Garage Band* • *SmartSound Sonic Fire* • Internet Browser
5. Preparing Image Media Resources	❑ Capturing digital video ❑ Converting video analog to digital ❑ Importing digital video ❑ Sizing images ❑ Resizing images for NTCS - TV format – not needed with *iPhoto* to *iMovie* feature ❑ Enhancing images for color, orientation, filters, cut-outs, special effects ❑ Creating image composites with text and other graphics ❑ Creating animations with layers	• Capturing digital video *with iMovie, VideoStudio 8, Final Cut or Premiere* • Importing digital video with *iMovie, VideoStudio 8, Final Cut or Premiere* • Resizing with *PhotoShop Elements* • Minimal enhancing with *iPhoto and Adobe Album* • Enhancing special effects with *ImageBlender* OR *Photoshop* • Creating image composites with *ImageBlender* OR *PhotoShop* • Creating animations with *VideoBlender, PhotoShop, VideoStudio 8, Final Cut or Premiere*,

Production Phase Gathering and Preparing Media Resources cont'd	Production Functions	BASIC Software Tools Used
5. Preparing Music/Sound Media Resources	❑ Equalizing ❑ Normalizing ❑ Trimming or cropping ❑ Extracting audio from video	• Equalizing, trimming and extracting sound features available with *iMovie*, *VideoStudio 8*, *Final Cut* or *Premiere* • *Bias Peak LE4* (MAC) or *Sound Forge* (WIN) needed for **advanced** features like normalizing voiceovers.

Post-Production Stage Putting it All Together	Post-Production Functions	BASIC Software Tools Used
6. Putting It All Together – BASIC video editing into full movie	❑ BASIC – Minimum features 2 audio tracks with 1 video track ❑ Audio capturing ❑ Frame grabbing from digital video ❑ Extracting sound from video ❑ Cropping video clips ❑ Cropping sound clips ❑ Adding animated and still titles to video and images ❑ Using Ken Burns still motion effects ❑ Adding transitions ❑ Drop and drag files directly into windows ❑ Ease of importing/exporting with format conversions ❑ Editing sound volume ❑ Editing time and speed of video / images ❑ Real-time rendering ❑ Real-time viewing w/ "scrubber"	• BASIC tracks found in *iMovie* (1 video + 2 audio) (MAC) and *VideoStudio 8* (2 video + 2 audio tracks) (WIN) • BASIC audio capturing with built-in computer recording used by *iMovie* (MAC) and *VideoStudio 8* (WIN) • BASIC editing features found in *iMovie* (MAC) and *VideoStudio 8* (WIN) Note: *MovieMaker 2* for PC Windows has ease of use and serves some purposes. But it definitely lacks a number of features that are considered essential or BASIC for digital storytelling. Some may choose to use it even with its limitations. It makes great photo essays.

Post-Production Phase
Putting it All Together

6. Putting It All Together – PRO video editing into full movie with additional high-end functions compared to BASIC functions

Post-Production Functions

❏ PRO features in addition to the BASIC features
❏ 99 video tracks
❏ 99 audio tracks
❏ In-program voice, audio, and sound capturing
❏ Animation
❏ Motion paths
❏ Rotating images
❏ Opacity
❏ Video composites
❏ Overlay objects / text
❏ Creating masks

PRO Software Tools Used

• PRO tracks (99 video + 99 audio) found in *Final Cut* (MAC) and *Premiere Express* (WIN)
• PRO audio capturing found in *Final Cut Express* (MAC), *Final Cut PRO* (MAC) and *Premiere Express* (WIN) and *Premiere* (WIN)

Distribution Phase
Applause! Applause!

7. Applause! Applause! Distribution as email, stand-alone movies, Internet files, DV streaming, DVD, and Bluetooth files for PDAs and cell phones.

Distribution Functions

❏ Direct export to camera
❏ Direct export to email
❏ Direct export to Internet websites
❏ Direct export to multiple file formats (qt, avi, rm)
❏ Direct export with chapter marks into DVD production programs
❏ Hollywood Style Special Effects: Selecting themes, sound tracks, interactive button styles, text styles, and drag/drop features)

BASIC Software Tools Used

Exporting into DVD production found in *iDVD* (MAC). *Final Cut* (MAC) also exports into *iDVD* production tools. Note: an Apple SuperDrive is needed to burn disks with *iDVD*.

If exporting onto DVD from *VideoStudio 8* and *Adobe Premiere*, special features that "dress-up" DVDs Hollywood style may be limited or not available depending on hardware configuration.

TIP: A number of WIN software programs import or export ONLY formats for Windows platforms rather than universal formats. Check file format exports carefully when choosing software IF you want to post and share files with others.

Chapter 7

Entering the Technical World of Digital Media

In the early stages of acquiring any really new skill, a person must adopt at least a partly antipleasure attitude by saying . . Yeah! GOOD! This is a chance to experience awkwardness and to discover new kinds of mistakes.

~ Marvin Minsky, The Society of Mind

Learning, Learning, Learning

Some feel the experience of using technology bewilderingly strange, like being in the Twilight Zone. Others find it an exhilarating time. Certainly for anyone new to using digital media, there are a lot of feelings that might come up when facing the learning curve of using multiple technical skills. On the other hand, creating a digital story is a perfect time to enjoy learning technical skills, especially if you are able to do this in a group setting. It is a matter of having a resourceful attitude towards learning PLUS having some support. Thankfully the newer technologies are now powerful and friendly enough that everyone from elementary students to grandparents can easily enter this technical world. This chapter provides basic technical information rather than specific software tutorials. A wealth of conventions, tips, ideas and resources are provided to help you get up to speed with some of the vocabulary and guidelines of using technology.

Learning is remembering what you are interested in.

~ Richard Wurman

Everyone is an Expert ~ Everyone is an Amateur

Many people who are just beginning to use technology tools may feel overwhelmed and look with envy at those who have already become "technology experts." But anyone who has a job requiring a lot of technical knowledge is painfully aware that they only know the smallest amount of what is possible to know. An odd paradox happens with gaining more technical skills: learning more only increases the awareness of what you don't know. So you are invited to graciously embrace a fundamental learning truth: the more you know, the more you know what you don't know. Patience will help you enjoy learning the technology you'll need for digital storytelling even more.

Education consists mainly of what we have unlearned.

~Mark Twain

I am learning all the time. The tombstone will be my diploma.

~ Eartha Kitt

This endless learning curve reminds me of my early experiences with learning a card game called Bridge. By understanding just a few simple rules, you can begin playing and hang in there having a good time with the best of them. You know what you know but don't know what you don't know – a great unconscious state of mind. But of course, the game is infinitely more complex than that. Over time I gradually learned many, many conventions and nuances that made me feel more expert but still I never stopped learning. At the end of each hand, the players at the table would review their cards, the bids and how they might have made a better game. This reflection process helped me gain more expertise over time. The good news for us all — you can play bridge (and technology) at both the entry level as well as the expert level and still enjoy the game.

It's not the hardware . . . It's the headware that will make our age truly great!

~ Ian Jukes

Don't strive to be an expert – just enjoy doing what you do with what you do know thus far. Don't judge or chide yourself — just learn what you need to know as you go along. Let your learning be guided by great questions in how to do what you want to do next. Over time skills will simply accumulate for you effortlessly.

Doubling Awareness of What You Don't Know

Here is an activity demonstrating the paradox of increasing what you know and what you don't know with any learning that you may do. Try drawing a line that represents to you the amount of knowledge you feel you have with technology right now. Regardless of how long it is, now draw a circle around the line. The line is the diameter and the circle around is the circumference. See Figure 1. The circumference drawn represents the amount of awareness of what you don't know that is created around the diameter of what you do know. Now imagine you are such a hot technology learner that you are able to double the length of the line every day. Draw a second line that is double the size of the first line drawn. NOW draw a circle around the second longer line. The space inside the circle now represents the amount of new awareness of what you don't know. See Figure 2.

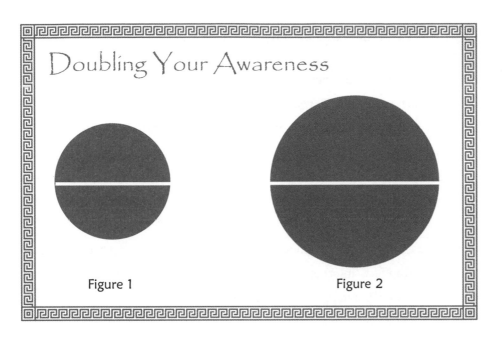

Doubling Your Awareness

Figure 1

Figure 2

Some people will never learn anything, for this reason, because they understand everything too soon.

~ Alexander Pope

You can appreciate after doing this activity that no matter how many technical skills you acquire over time, there will always, always be more to learn. So don't stress yourself comparing what you know to others. You know what you need to know until you are ready to know more. The good news of experiencing digital storytelling is that it demystifies technology while giving you an opportunity to increase technical skills using the focus of acquiring the art of personal storytelling.

I do not think much of a man who does not know more today than he did yesterday.

~ Abraham Lincoln

Featured Resource:
e-Learning at Atomic Learning.

Atomic Learning is a subscription website to help people learn technical skills visually with movie tutorials. Various software functions for both MAC and PC WINDOWS are demonstrated in small movie clips. It is a great way to ease into learning a product by selecting just one movie or concept at a time. A number of their movie clips are available at no charge. Check it out! (www.atomiclearning.com)

Start With Being Copyright Savvy

The gumball machine broke and all the gumballs are rolling down the floor.

~ Howard E. King, attorney representing lawsuits against Napster, 2000

Do you know the copyright guidelines for using digitized media resources? Before using any resource, check out copyright and fair use laws along with guidelines for citation of resources. There are ethical considerations as well as legal liabilities in using intellectual property that belongs to someone else. Just because it is on the Web and CAN be downloaded doesn't make it yours any more than scanning or digitizing images or music gives you usage rights.

There are a wide range of technologies available to gather and prepare media elements: scanners, Internet sites, digital still cameras, software that allows translating video/music/sound from analog to digital, capturing digital movies, and digitizing voice or music. If you are leading a digital storytelling workshop or working with other groups, be sure that you have all participants sign permission slips that also ask them to vouch for clearing any copyrights in their digital stories. See a sample permission form under DigiTales' Resources Extra! Extra! (www.digitales.us)

Review Stanford's University Libraries (http://fairuse.stanford.edu) where you will find an extensive Web resource of copyright, fair use and intellectual property topics related to text and digital media. Teachers and students will also want to check out Hall Davidson's Website (www.halldavidson.net) for a PDF summary chart of the fair use guidelines for classrooms. Invest time as you go in documenting any information sources you use so that you will be ready to develop the credits screens at the end of your story.

TIP: How well can you interpret copyright laws? For fun you might want to take Hall Davidson's copyright quiz. (www.halldavidson.net)

TIP: Use David Warlick's online Citation Machine to easily organize citations for all types of resources. (www.landmark-project.com) David also includes a number of easy-to-use forms to use for getting formal permission to legally use copyrighted materials.

Organizing Project Folders

In the pre-production phase of making a digital story, it was recommended that you organize your project folders. If you have not done this yet, you will want to set those up right now. Create a project folder with your name if computers are being shared. Make an additional six subfolders (subdirectories) to put inside your project folder. Do NOT move these folders or files out of the original project folder. Review Step Three in *Chapter 5: Stepping Through Making a Digital Story* (p.130).

Creating a Voiceover

Voiceovers are personal narratives performed and digitized from a written story script. Think of your voice recording as a "performance" rather than a reading. You need to be in the story – feeling it – living it – breathing it and sharing it from the heart as an experience only YOU can know. Vary the pace and tone in ways that shift with the story's meaning. Soothe the listener in moments that are tranquil. Put voice energy into moments of excitement. Leave pauses or punctuations that build the climax and tension. Make room in your voice delivery for any "guest" voices or stand-alone sounds that were storyboarded from your music/sound lists. Practice out loud or read your script to others prior to recording. Rehearsing will help you develop a rhythm for the story. Trust your own approach and your natural voice to make the story your own.

Don't say the old lady screamed-bring her on and let her scream.

~ Mark Twain

VoiceOver File Protocols

Name your files with the following alphabetical protocol. This naming protocol will facilitate the importing of the voiceover chunks into your digital story as if it was one continuous reading in which the voice flows seamlessly together.

Sample File Naming:

a_storyname

b_storyname

c_storyname

After using the storyboard planning process to ensure that you have exactly the script you want to use, you are ready to record your voiceover. The good news is the digitizing process of developing a voiceover allows you ample opportunity to record multiple takes of the reading until you have what you like.

It is recommended you divide the script up into several sentences or paragraph "chunks" by literally adding physical spaces in your writing where there are natural pauses or shifts in the story. Record each "chunk" separately. This way if you choose to re-record, you have only a "chunk" to do over rather than the pressure of flawlessly performing the entire script again in one take. Use the voiceover file protocols to organize each recording in alphabetical order. When they are placed together on the audio track, they will read seamlessly using your natural pauses to make file transitions unnoticeable between files.

PRO VoiceOver Recording Station ~ Approximately $400

- Bias Peak 4LE software (MAC)
- Sound Forge software (WIN)
- M-Audio Mobile Pre USB (audio interface w/ computer)
- Condenser microphone (Shure)
- Boom Stand
- Aspiration (spit) Guard

There are a variety of methods to digitize voices. It is important to balance which tools and software you choose with being able to digitize at the highest quality possible. Begin with a quiet room to eliminate any distracting background noises. An external microphone with a spit guard will create better voice sound than using the computer's built-in microphone. Some video-editing software may be able to capture sounds and voices but are so basic that there are not specific controls to increase or decrease the volume being captured or adjust it afterwards (equalizing or normalizing). Without adjustment controls, the voice quality is what it is when you capture it. Watch the audiometers on the computer screen for a visual display of the sound level. If the software does not allow adjusting, test a small sample reading to determine if your voice is too loud or too soft until you have it just right. Keep checking the clarity and sound level of the digitized voice and re-record until you have a quality voiceover.

Evaluate yourself by your own standards, not someone else's.

~ Anonymous

Video-editing software programs (*Final Cut, VideoStudio 8, and Premiere*) do provide limited volume and sound adjustment features that will work in most cases. An external microphone is still recommended rather than the internal microphones on most computers. If you are going to create a number of digital stories or work with groups, it is recommended that you consider PRO level audio capturing software: *Bias Peak 4LE* (MAC) or *Sound Forge* (WIN). The hardware together with PRO audio software creates very professional, clear voiceovers. Detailed directions for capturing voiceovers with *Bias Peak 4LE* software including normalizing the voice can be found at DigiTales' Resources Extra! Extra! (www.digitales.us)

TIP: Record in a quiet room to eliminate picking up distracting background noises.

TIP: Equalizing increases or decreases the level of smaller portions of certain frequencies. Normalizing increases the overall volume of an audio recording to maximum volume without distorting it. Normalizing is a feature of PRO audio software that adjusts the quality of the entire file at the same time.

TIP: The normalizing feature is highly recommended if a digital story has multiple voices. Normalizing will enable you to make each voice file have the same sound balance rather than one voice being strong and another voice being soft.

How do I know what I think until I see what I say.

~ E.M. Forster

Scanning Images

Getting existing images digitized into your computer usually means having a scanner. There are many kinds of scanners but flatbed scanners are the most common. *Adobe Photoshop* is the most popular software used to scan the images into the computer. Having the image scanned into *Photoshop* means you can size and edit it in real time. However, some scanners come with their own software. General guidelines or tips provided here will apply to most

Ideas for Scanning Images

Scanning can be a creative experience. Try some of these objects. If you have a large or awkward object, try taking a photo using a digital camera rather than wrestling with the scanner.

Old photos	Greeting cards
Report cards	Watches
Fabric	Jewelry
Post cards	Letters
Papers	Flowers or leaves
Book covers	Hair braids
Drawings	Mementos
Art work	Wall paper

scanners. Be sure to check the documentation for the scanner and software for more specific instructions.

If computers get too powerful, we can organize them into a committee — that will do them in.

~ Bradley's Bromide.

Understanding Image Resolution

There is a lot of jargon and a number of conventions to learn concerning digital imaging. One of the most important concepts to understand is resolution, which determines the quality of the image. Resolution required for printing is different than what is needed for video screens or Web pages. The higher the resolution, the more detail you will see and the more memory will be required for each image file. Higher resolution images also take more time to process in software programs. If the resolution is too low, especially for smaller images that you expect to scale up or make larger, the image will appear jagged or "bit mapped." You want quality images but not any higher quality than you need. The scanning resolution you choose needs to be based on which output device is processing the image as well as the size of the original object being scanned.

Printers use a resolution measured in dots-per-inch (dpi). Dpi determines the quality of the image on paper. If you are scanning images for fine books you will need a very dense image quality of **600 to 1200** dpi. If you are printing scanned images to a printer, **150** dpi will create a quality resolution on paper.

Video screens use resolutions measured in pixels-per-inch (ppi). The term pixel is an abbreviation for picture elements. Optimal pixel resolution is **720x534.** This provides the quality needed at 100% scale – meaning you will be using the image at the same size that it is captured. While inches describe what images look like on paper, pixels describe what images will look like on video screens. Even thought ppi is the technical term to express video resolution, scanning software options and manuals usually identify this type of resolution as dpi as well.

The size of the image needs to be factored into the resolution needed. If you are scanning images for video screens, **200 dpi** will likely provide sufficient quality if the picture used is left at 100% scale. Scale means not enlarging or shrinking the original image size. If the pixel size (ppi) of the image is 720x534 then it will likely not need enlarging as this is the size and quality needed to fill a video screen. If the images being scanned are quite small (postage stamps) or you expect to scale or enlarge them from the original size, then scan the image at **300 dpi**. Many people prefer to scan all their images at **300 dpi** to have the resolution they need for enlarging, cropping, or creating high quality cut-outs (taking one portion or selection out of the image). Keep in mind that if you are scanning color images at 300 dpi you'll need a lot of memory on your hard drive. For example, scanning a color 8.5 x 11 image at 300 dpi requires 25 megabytes of memory. Larger image files also slow down processing time in software programs.

TIP: Very detailed scanning information is available for those wanting more technical guidelines. (www.scantips.com)

TIP: NTSC (National Television Standards Committee) is the standard format used in the USA and PAL (Phase Alternating Line) is the standard format used in Europe, Asia, Africa, etc. The pixel resolution differs creating a different proportion between the width and height of the image. For example NTSC uses **640 x 480** and PAL uses **768 x576**.

Getting Images from Cameras

Still digital cameras are plentiful these days. These cameras can generally be plugged directly into a computer's USB port for images to download into your photo software (*iPhoto or Adobe PhotoAlbum*). Like scanned images, camera photos are measured in pixel resolutions. Entry-level cameras typically provide at least two (2) megapixel resolution. A camera with four (4) to five (5) megapixel resolution gives you higher quality images for editing and publishing the images. Camera settings range from low resolution photos that can easily be emailed to family and friends to high resolution photos that produce the higher quality images needed for video production. If still digital cameras are set to the highest resolution, memory storage cards will generally hold two photos per megabyte. Many digital still cameras also have a range of special settings to take photos of text, micro images and wide angle shots including panoramas.

If you are using a traditional camera, you can request that a Photo CD to be made along with your regular prints. The Photo CD images usually come in more than one resolution, offering both low quality images that are good enough to email and high quality images for printing and use in video on the same disk.

Just because something doesn't do what you planned it to do doesn't mean it's useless.

~ Thomas Edison

TIP: If you do not have a scanner, you can use a still digital camera to shoot your object for an immediate image, or by planning ahead, use a traditional camera to get digital images on a Photo CD.

TIP: Digital movie cameras have become very affordable and portable. Most of them use firewire cables to download movies into computers at very high speeds. There are some very interesting digital movie cameras being made for kids today that cost under $100, such as the *Blue Digital Movie Creator* that can be found at Toys R US stores. The package includes a USB cable and is only PC compatible at this time. You can only record up to four (4) minutes of video, so you would have to splice and dice a lot of pieces together. But this product shows a trend in getting digital camera tools directly into the hands of kids. And adults are now ready to join them. Get more details on digital camera shopping.
(http://members.ozemail.com.au/~leemshs/digvideo.htm#Planning)

TIP: For additional information on camera basics and file transferring between cameras and computers, visit Tech4Learning's tutorial and tips.
(www.tech4learning.com/snacks/dcameras.html)

Video is generally imported directly into your video-editing software (*iMovie, Ulead's VideoStudio 8, Final Cut* or *Premiere*). Most software packages feature the option to automatically start a new clip at each scene break, which means identifying the place when the camera was turned on or off. Because video uses a LOT of memory, so downloading the entire film footage before trimming and deleting doesn't make much sense. You will want to import only selected video clip scenes so you do no overload your memory space. If you are using a shot list described in pre-production phase, you will have exactly what you need for your storyboard to have only the video clips that you need.

TIP: Preview the video first. Select video clips that are no longer than 5-15 seconds long. Grab a couple of seconds of video before and after the exact scene that you expect to use. This leave "handles" on either side of the clip to use with transitions or other special effects. The extra video can always be trimmed or cropped later in the video-editing software.

TIP: If you do not have access to a digital video camera, you can convert VHS tapes using an analog to digital converter box. The converter box has VCR jacks for input and USB output to the computer. The analog to digital video device allows the video to be captured by the software in the same way as a digital camera is connected to the computer.

TIP: Downloading video uses a LOT of memory. It requires 3.6 megabyte per second or one (1) gigabyte of memory for every five (5) minutes of digitized video. If you plan to use a lot of video, you will want an additional 200+ gigabyte external hard drive.

TIP: Use a large piece of black velvet fabric on a wall as a backdrop for interviews or moving objects.

TIP: Use a digital movie camera to record quality voices or sounds. It creates a better sound than using some built-in computer microphones. You can extract the voice from the video with most video-editing software packages (*iMovie*, *Ulead's VideoStudio 8*, *Final Cut*, and *Premiere*)

When life is a gift, open it; a joy, share it; a pleasure, have some; a game, play it; a joke, laugh; an experience, live it; a story, tell it true!

~ Anonymous

Getting Images from the Web

There are lots of Websites that offer free clipart, graphics, animations, photographs, or images for private non-commercial use. Sometimes the images are completely free. Other sites have legitimate "free" resources but require you to create an "account" by registering first. Beware! Your email address will now likely be used for marketing. Some of these companies trade their resources for access to your name, address and/or email. I usually have a legitimate but empty email address for these situations. This empty email is usually Web-based and mail to this address is not sent directly to my desktop.

Other Websites offer **royalty-free resources**. Companies that provide royalty-free images or music / sounds usually ask that you pay a subscription fee to access and use their entire collections. Sometimes there is a price per item that is put in the "cart." There are no restrictions on usage or further fees required on royalty-free resources. All of the sites listed below give away a portion of their collection as a marketing strategy to entice subscribers to use their services. Enjoy the many "free" samples in these sites or if you find a great site, the subscription fee may be worth paying.

Download images through your Internet browser. To search the entire Web for an image you need, use Googles' search engine. (www.google.com) Click on the word "Images" just above the search line and then enter the keyword for the image you are looking to download. If you type in "cow," you will now only find images of cows rather than all references including text articles. This image search will present a number of "thumbnails" of the images that match your keyword.

Check the pixel dimension under each picture. You will want an image resolution with at least **720 x 534 pixels.** Lesser resolutions will work if the image will be part of a composite (combined with other images) or used in a small portion of the screen's image. Otherwise, if you use an image that is less than **720 x534** pixels, the resolution quality will not be high enough for you to enlarge it to fill the entire video screen without degradation. It is noted that some people do use images with pixel resolutions of **500 to 600** ppi, realizing that the image may not be the best but the photo is exactly what they were looking for.

You can also do a general Internet search by putting in the file format tag (.PICT or .JPEG or .MOV) in the search line after the item you are wanting with a plus (+) sign as part of your criteria (for example, enter the keyword cow + .PIC).

TIP: Many Web graphics are only **72** dpi. Animated gifs are also created as very low resolution graphics. While this low resolution is perfect for saving memory and easing downloading demands, these same images will be give very low quality in video productions.

Image Web Resources to Explore

www.pics4learning.com

http://office.microsoft.com/clipart

www.animation-station.com

www.barrysclipart.com

www.backgroundcity.com

http://memory.loc.gov

www.clipart.com

www.fresherimage.com

www.FreeFoto.com

www.ulead.com/download/freedownload.htm

www.free-photographs.net

www.FreeGraphics.org

www.fresherimage.com

www.stockedphotos.com

Getting information off the Internet is like taking a drink from a fire hydrant.

~ Mitchell Kapor

TIP: Be sure to read the terms of use at any site from which you are taking images or sounds since many require you to include screen credits to the authors or Websites as part of your permission to use the resources. It is a good practice at any rate to cite all sources of any resources you use.

TIP: Before you download the image, be sure to click on the image's thumbnail to view the actual size image. Otherwise you will be downloading the very low resolution and size thumbnail image.

TIP: You can save images to your desktop by holding down the mouse on the MAC for a few seconds to give you a pop-up window and then select the option called SAVE IMAGE AS. You can then choose a file name and location for your image. You get the same choices by using right mouse clicking on an image using PC Windows functions. Direct these image files to the IMAGE folder located in your PROJECT's folder.

Saving Image File Formats

As you save your image files, you will be asked for a file name and what file format you want to use. Format files vary in quality. **JPEG** (Joint Photographic Experts Group) is the most common format. But because JPEG compresses the files – shrinking the size by discarding information – it lowers the file size and the image quality. **PICT** format uses less compression therefore having higher image quality. This format works well for most image needs. **TIFF** format (Tagged Image File Format) was designed to be independent of hardware platforms as an industry standard for image-file exchange. Most software programs can now use this high quality image format. If you are using Photoshop as your scanning software, you can leave your image file in its native format called **PSD**. PSD files can be imported without conversion into *iPhoto* and *Adobe Photo Album* as well as a variety of video editing software packages. Direct these image files to the IMAGE folder located in your PROJECT's folder.

One machine can do the work of fifty ordinary men. No machine can do the work of one extraordinary man.

~ Elbert Hubbard, The Roycroft Dictionary and Book of Epigrams, 1923

Image File Format Vocabulary

AVI – an Audio Video InterLeave format for audio AND video files. This is the most common format for audio/video data on the PC. These are highly compressed and very transportable movies. MAC computers can read and use these files with *iTunes*, *iMovie*, and *QuickTime* software.

DV Stream – Digital Video Streaming uses a 5:1 compression scheme for movies and can manage sharp edges and vivid colors.

GIF (.gif) – a Graphic Interchange Format used to create web images. It saves images with a very limited number of colors that makes this format a low quality for print and video. No special viewers are required for this file format by either computer platform.

JPEG (.jpeg) – a Joint Photographic Experts' Group used for images. JPEGS are generally compressed files that are easy to transfer but lose resolution when compressed creating lower quality. No special viewers needed.

MPEG 4 (.mpg) – a Motion Picture Experts Group movie file format. These are higher resolution and better quality than QuickTime versions. You need a high-speed computer to download and view. The average file size for the .mpg format is about nine megabytes for each minute of motion picture. However, while these files are great for distribution, they are not able to be imported into editing programs. This means you will not be able to do editing such as extracting audio or video with any files that are MPEG format.

QuickTime (.qt) – a QuickTime file video format for movies. This format offers the ability to view smaller, downloadable files as well as enhanced image, higher resolution files depending upon how they are saved. This format can be read by both platforms with free *QuickTime Readers*.

RealMedia (.rm) – a RealMedia movie format file useful for computers connected to the Internet via phone line and modem. The movie can be viewed as it arrives at your computer eliminating the need to download the movie completely before viewing. Video playback is slower and may be affected by Internet traffic. MAC computers need the free *RealOne Player* and WIN computers need *Media Player* installed.

TIFF (.tiff) – a Tagged Image File Format. These are high-resolution images and therefore larger file sizes than .gif or .jpeg images. TIFF images are usually used by high end page layouts, for presentations, and movie making.

TIP: Generally you will want to use either a PICT or TIFF format to ensure quality images.

Editing Images

After gathering your images, you will find that some may be exactly what you want therefore needing no editing at all. Other images may need simple cropping or trimming to take out unwanted visuals or to grab just a small portion of the image to create a close-up. An image may also need the color, contrast, brightness, red eyes, or clarity repaired. You can also change an image by adding text or special visual effects. Or perhaps you will want to create a still composite by combining one or more images into a custom visual. BASIC editing functions are provided by *iPhoto and Adobe Photo Album* software, including cropping, auto color or red-eye repair, changing color to black and white or sepia tones, contrast, brightness or rotating. Tech4Learning's *ImageBlender* give more editing features (text, shapes, composites, and drawing) than *iPhoto* and *Adobe Photo Album* which beginners welcome if they are not quite ready for *Photoshop*.

Advanced Image Editing

Advanced or PRO level editing requires using software like *Adobe Photoshop Elements*. Consider adding text titles or key words onto images. While this effect can be done by using titles, you have many more options for the look and feel you want to accomplish by using *Photoshop*. However, *Adobe Photo Album* does allow you to add text to images.

Making composites can be time consuming but you are able to create some unique images. A composite is built by taking an image from one image file and then pasting it into another image file. You might think of composites as a collage. Identify the image you want, select the magnetic lasso to surround the object, feather it to blend better with new background, and then cut and paste the object into new image. Each image you combine creates a "layer" in the photo that can be moved and edited separately. You can place people in new backgrounds (your brother's picture from a family picnic selected and pasted along side other astronauts on a space shuttle), add objects (putting a vase of roses on the table), make a collage (a scanned letter with an oval image of the writer placed on top) or perhaps resize a selected image (a fly) to be very, very large or very small in proportion to other objects. There is also a photomerge function that arranges any combination of photos you choose into a panorama.

You can also use the magnetic lasso to make cut-out objects useful to develop animation IF you are using a video editing programs with two (2) or more video tracks (*Final Cut Pro*, *Ulead's VideoStudio 8*, or *Adobe's Premiere*). For example, you can select a star that will be placed on a second video track above the image of an open hand that has been placed on the first video track. The star image object overlays the hand image but appears only when you command it to appear. You can then sequence the images so the movie starts with the empty open hand and then have the star dissolve into the hand. This strategy allows you to move objects in and out of image scenes. It also allows you to move objects in an animated path, such as having a moon moving quickly across the sky above grandpa's front porch. Using cut-outs for this visual effect is fun and creative once you learn this advanced process.

Masks are shapes that have holes in them. They are used as overlays – an image with a hole that lays over another still or moving image. You can see through the holes to what is placed behind the mask. With this technique, you can get some wild and exciting effects. Try large cut out letters with a movie of an ocean surf playing behind them. Or maybe using a face of a lion with its mouth cut out that plays a video of a real person's moving lips behind it. Or maybe something as simple as a television screen or other interesting frame that has the middle removed to mask (overlay) on top of a favorite still image or movie.

The factory of the future will have only two employees, a man and a dog. The man will be there to feed the dog. The dog will be there to keep the man from touching the equipment.

~ Warren G. Bennis

There are many, many more special effects possible with *Adobe Photoshop Elements*. While all these special effects are quite fun, remember to keep your first projects simple; stay with the basics. Or if you have a lot of learning fortitude, plunge into using some advanced image editing tools using *Adobe Photoshop Elements*.

TIP: Lisa Lee has a great visual resource book with step-by-step directions called *How to Use Photoshop Elements 2.* Her two page lessons using color graphics are very easy to use.

TIP: Many special image effects can be created within the video-editing programs such as creating video within video (picture within picture) scenes using transitions and special effects. Eric Sadun's book, *iMovie 3 Solutions* is a great MAC resource with advanced tips, tricks and special effects for *iMovie* and *QuickTime Pro*.

TIP: Another interesting advanced visual special effect is the process of transforming one image into another called morphing. For example, morph the older image version of grandma into a younger one. Or an old house can be morphed into a new house image. This is a fun, artistic way of expressing change.

Sizing Images

Are your images the right size for the screen? It is a matter of understanding aspect ratio. Television or computer monitor displays use a **4x3** aspect ratio. It is possible that your images were scanned, captured or downloaded with just the size you need to fill the screen. You may not need to size images at all. That is why understanding resolution for scanning and downloading is important. If images are opened in *Adobe Photoshop*, the bottom of the image's window will state the pixel resolution. The resolution size needs to be **720x534 pixels** in order to fill the entire screen. This is a **4x3** ratio with enough image information to produce a quality image. If images are imported into video-editing software without sizing them to a 4x3 ratio, black bars will generally show around the image to make up the extra viewing space.

The good news for *iPhoto* users is the program's ability to translate images automatically into *iMovie* and *iDVD*. Use *iPhoto* images just as you have captured them or crop the images in the editing feature using the 4x3 contrain ratio. *iPhoto* also alerts you to substandard images that will display distorted or pixilated. Either way, the computer mathematically translates each *iPhoto* image to fill the screen when imported into *iMovie*. PC Window users will have additional steps to size any images that are not in the correct resolution or aspect ratio. Fortunately, images placed in *Adobe Photo Album* are easily transported into *Adobe Photoshop*. Here images can be sized to **720x534** and then resaved as PICT resource or TIFF format files into your project's IMAGE folder located on your desktop.

TIP: MAC users need to put all collected images into *iPhoto* first to take advantage of the automatic sizing and squashing features for *iMovie* and *iDVD*.

TIP: WIN users will need to use *Adobe Photoshop* to size all images.

TIP: When enlarging images, it is important to start with high quality pixel resolution. If you do decide to enlarge an image, the image quality will be better retained if you enlarge by increments rather than all at once. For example, if you want to double the size of an image, do it 110% at a time rather than jumping directly to 200%. First increase the image to 110 percent, then save. Now increase the new image another 110 percent. This can be time consuming but it will help save the resolution quality because the computer has more information each time to work with when filling in the missing pixels as you double the image.

Resizing Images

Just because something doesn't do what you planned it to do doesn't mean it's useless.

~ Thomas Alva Edison

Beware, there is still more math to understand because computers generally use square pixels while television and broadcast video use rectangular pixels. If you do not resize your images, what you see on the computer screen will be distorted on the television screen. What may be a circle on your computer screen may show up as an oval on the television screen if you don't go through the process of resizing images for this difference. This resizing is called "squashing."

Images are resized by squashing or squeezing down the pixels before using them in your video editing software. MAC users will want to take advantage of *iPhoto's* automatic pixel squashing by making sure all images are first placed in the *iPhoto* program. When *iPhotos* are brought into *iMovie* or *iDVD*, the computer is programmed to automatically resize or squash images pixels from computer screen resolution (**720X534**) to television screen resolution (**640X480**) without requiring any extra user steps.

PC Window users will need to resize all images that were digitized, scanned, or downloaded from the Internet. Resizing is done in *Adobe Photoshop* by selecting the entire sized image and then changing the sized images from the **720x534** pixels to **640x480** pixels. These resized images need to be saved in the project's IMAGESEDITED folder on the desktop. The resolution of these "squashed" images is now ready for PC video-editing software.

TIP: All PC users will need to use *Adobe Photoshop* to re-size all images.

TIP: The folder named IMAGESEDITED is meant to store all final images ready to go for post-production after they have been edited or resized.

Getting Music and Sounds from CDs

All Music CDs can be imported by sound editing programs like *iTunes*, *Sound Tracks*, *Ulead's VideoStudio 8*, *Final Cut*, and *Premiere*. Using *iTunes* makes this process very simple. Simply put the disk into the computer. You can either import the entire disk from within the *iTunes* program or click and drag individual tracks onto the *iTunes* window. The music and sounds are now part of the *iTunes* library. Again be aware of copyrighted soundtracks and purchase and/or get permission for their use.

Making Customized Music and Sound

Since only a few of us feel we are musicians, using copyrighted songs seemed to be our only choice. But there is no longer a need to even consider stepping over the legal lines. The **DigiTales Toolkit** includes a fabulously fun resource from *Smart Sound* available for both platforms. Using either *SmartSounds' Movie Maestro or Sonic Fire Pro*, making music sound tracks is now fast and fun. You can import your movie into Smart Sound to place soundtracks in real time with the video. Or you can create and export sound tracks usable in the video-editing software programs. Many, many additional music libraries are available to vary your choices.

Other programs like Apple's *GarageBand* let you mix and match music loops for endless music tracks composed by your very own Bach self. It is a great opportunity to increase your music intelligence by practicing the art of making your own instrumental soundtracks. You can even add in lyrics or vocal sounds with your own voice.

Getting Music and Sounds from the Internet

Like the image Websites, some sites include free music and sound resources. Some companies have "free" resources if you sign up for an account at no charge. But beware that your email address and name frequently will likely become part of a marketing list. You are selling your name for free resources. Other companies have royalty-free resources, which means you pay a subscription fee to use the entire library for non-commercial purposes. They usually offer sample free music and sound resources to entice you to consider subscribing. Be sure to read the terms. And subscribe to anything that you feel is worth the annual fee.

You can also find music and sound resources through your Internet browser. To search the entire Web for a piece of music or sound that you need, use Google's search engine. (www.google.com) Enter the keyword for the type of music/sound you are wanting to download. For example, if you type in "cow" plus "sound" (cow + sound) you will now only find sounds of cows rather than all references including text articles.

Music and Sound Web Resources to Explore

http://wavcentral.com

http://sounddogs.com

www.hollywoodedge.com/the/

www.partnersinrhyme.com/pir/PIRsfx.html

www.midiworld.com/sounds.htm#samples

www.mp3advance.com

TIP: The file format on a Website may appear on the screen to be a QuickTime file. However if you click on the far right down triangle for your saving options, you can choose SAVE as SOURCE rather than saving as a QuickTime movie file. Source means the sound saves as an original sound in WAV or AIFF file format.

TIP: If you download a file in a format that doesn't import into your video-editing software, use *QuickTime Pro* to convert the file to a useable format.

TIP: MAC users: import all sound files into *iTunes*.

TIP: It is a good practice to cite all sources of any resources you use. Be sure to read the terms of use at any site from which you are taking music or sounds since many require that you include screen credits listing the authors or Websites as part of your permission to use the resources. Other sites limit the use of their work to only personal use which means no distribution of any kind – Web, DVD's etc.

Technology is no place for wimps!

~ Scott Raymond Adams, Creator of Dilbert

Editing Music and Sound Files

The most common editing needed for music and sound files are cropping and splitting functions. Cropping means you only want to use a portion of the sound file. You identify or select which section you want and then delete the rest of the sound. Splitting means making two or more separate pieces out of one soundtrack. Generally you place the "scrubber" or playhead at the place you want to trim and then use a tool from the edit menu to literally split the soundtrack or sound. This now makes two pieces of sound images. You can now move the pieces around separately or highlight and delete the piece you no longer want. Being able to visually see the waveforms (visual representation of the sounds) for these tasks is very helpful. *iTunes* does not have these sound editing functions. But all video-editing software in the DigiTales Toolkits can trim, split or crop sounds.

Music and Sound File Format Vocabulary

ACC – Advance Audio Coding for audio files. This is a cutting edge audio code perfect for the Internet, offering high-quality sound in smaller file sizes. ACC compresses more efficiently than older formats such as MP3. It is virtually undistinguishable from the original uncompressed audio source.

AIFF – an Audio Interchange Format File for audio files. Provides high quality music and sound formats. This is *iMovie's* native format. Any imported sound file will automatically be converted into AIFF format. This format lets you extract the sound track from your *iMovie* and save to a sound-only file format. And it can also be read by Window's *Media Player*.

AVI – an Audio Video InterLeave format for audio AND video files. This is the most common format for audio/video data on the PC. These are highly compressed and very transportable movies. MAC computers can read and use these files with *iTunes*, *iMovies*, and *QuickTime* software.

MP3 (MAC and WIN) – a high-quality audio sound format that comes close to the quality of WaveForm (.wav) at greatly reduced file size. Depending on the players, these files are sometimes tinny depending on the bit rate which is how much information is going by per second. MP3 files need to be at least 128 kbps for quality sound. However, these compressed files download much faster than .wav files. MAC computers need QuickTime and WIN computers need *Media Player* installed.

QT (MAC and WIN) – these are *QuickTime* files. This format can be audio only or a video format for movies. It offers the ability to view smaller, downloadable files as well as enhanced image, higher resolution files depending upon how the files are saved. This format can be read by both platforms using *QuickTime Readers*.

RealAudio (MAC and WIN) – delivers fast audio sound with a minimum of download time. It is a low quality format and cannot be changed or converted in any way once it is downloaded. MAC and WIN computers need to have *RealOne Player* installed.

WaveForm (.wav) – these are cross platform files (MAC and WIN). WAV files are high-quality audio sound files. Download time is longer than other audio formats. These files must be downloaded completely before they can be played. MAC computers need *QuickTime* and WIN computers need *Media Player* installed.

WMA (Windows Media Audio) – this audio file runs on the PC Windows platform only.

Another editing feature is adjusting the volume of the sound clip. This is useful when you want a strong opening or closing but don't want to drown out another sound or compete with your voiceover. Adjustments in sound levels can also be made for fade in and fade out effects with a sound clip. Generally a marker is place on the sound track line and then pulled up or down to adjust the sound level.

TIP: Some video-editing programs let you turn the sound tracks into visual audio waves – try preferences! This allows more precise editing.

TIP: Another useful sound editing feature is the ability to extract the sound from a movie clip. AIFF format is great for this feature. Separating or extracting the video from the audio track lets you use only the sound with other images or only the video with a different soundtrack.

TIP: *The DigiCam Chronicles: Sound is Half the Picture* (MAC) by Derrick Story has great ideas and tips for using and enchancing audio capture, making audio postcards, great voice overs and screenshot animations. (www.macdevcenter.com/pub/a/mac/2003/01/28/digicam_chronicles.html)

Multimedia? As far as I'm concerned, it's reading with the radio on.

~ Andrew Brown

Saving Sound File Formats

The two most common sound formats are WAV or AIFF. Both these file types are high quality formats that can be used across platforms. MP3 files are compression files that need to be formatted with a minimum of 128 kbps otherwise they can have a "tinny" low quality sound. ACC is a new audio code generally used with iPods. It is a new compression format designed to deliver a higher quality sound.

TIP: Use *iTunes* to manage both sound and music files. You can create sound playlists that let you more easily locate files according to category.

Using Transitions and Special Effects

All elements like titles, transitions, and special effects should be chosen to extend the impact of the message or story rather than being used as "eye candy" or decoration. Most video-editing software has a multitude of choices for adding transitions (e.g., barn doors, wipe right, fly-in, cube, radial, flap or vortex) and special effects (shrink and dissolve, earthquake, flash, fog or fairy dust). You can also purchase additional transition and special effets to add to your video-editing software's library.

TIP: Transitions are the actions that happen between images. Special effects are the qualities that are overlayed on top of an image thereby changing an original image.

Experiment, explore and enjoy! However, just because you can make your picture spin off the page doesn't mean you should. Having all these choices provides us with the same kind of fun we had when discovering you can make your word processing documents have 99 different fonts. The first tendency is to playfully use a lot of different font types, styles, sizes and colors. It is fun and interesting. But it also created a ransom note look. Rather than engaging your audience in the power of your story, so many variations actually distract and disengage viewers.

Transitions and special effects are powerful IF they visually contribute to unfolding the story. A barn door transition might be chosen to open up onto a garden scene. A radial transition could be used to represent time passing. A closing heart special effect might represent the end of a heart-warming relationship. The push transition can give a feel of animation letting an image lead the viewer into another scene.

Transitions and special effects are the last element added to your images. When they are inserted they are "taped" to the left and right sides of the images. The transitions and special effects actually take up a portion of the visual space on either side. If the duration or length of time of either image is set too short, there may not be enough room for the transition to operate.

Unless you are going for a very special visual message, keep transitions simple and consistent so they don't overshadow your story. The fade-in transition traditionally starts a story, while a fade-out ends the story, followed by the credits. Cross dissolves are the most commonly used transitions between scenes. But you may find moving from scene to scene without transitions may just give images the right story tone. Consider these general guidelines, but feel free to experiment with your own style while noticing how each transition or special effect does or does not develop your story.

In Conclusion

Learn a little. Learn a lot. Technology skills should be learned as needed. It is the way you will really remember them long term. It is highly recommended to create initial digital stories in groups. Helping and problem-solving together makes the learning curves more manageable and doable.

I don't need an instruction manual, I'm perfectly capable of screwing it up without printed help, thank you.

~ Author unknown

Chapter 8

Extra! Extra!
Resources for Digital Storytelling

In China (around the time of Christ), writers were recording their notes on slips of bamboo. The slips of bamboo were held together with silk. The intellect of a scholar was judged on how many carts it took to carry all his books when he took a journey.

~ Frank Granger

Lots of Carts for Your Storytelling Journey

This book was created through the many good works, experiences and thinking of others who have gone before me. I built my interest, understandings and experiences from so many wise and caring people – some I have met and others yet strangers. While I have credited authors for their ideas, you may find yourself wanting more than a sample taste of their thinking and ideas. The following books, articles, and Websites provide additional resources for the topics and ideas discussed in DigiTales.

Disclaimer for Websites

Many Website addresses are not always sustained for a variety of reasons. The Websites listed in the book chapters were working as listed when this book went to press. It is entirely possible that a few may no longer be available over time. I will keep an ongoing, updated list of resources at www.digitales.us.

If a man has come to that point where he is so content that he says; I do not want to know any more, or do any more or be any more, he is in a state of which he ought to be changed into a mummy.

~ Henry Ward Beecher

Articles

- Banaszewski, Tom. "Storytelling Finds It Place in the Classroom." (www.infotoday.com/MMSchools/jan02/banaszewski.htm)

- Story-Time Blues' "The Use of Story to Create Learning and Community." (www.goodshare.org/storyblu.htm)

- Mamie Marcuss' "The New Community Anthology: Digital Storytelling." (www.bos.frb.org/commdev/c&b/2003/fall/digital.pdf)

> I find that a great part
> of the information I
> have was acquired by
> looking up something
> and finding something
> else on the way.
>
> ~ Franklin P. Adams

> When I read that the
> best way to preserve a
> book is to not read it; I
> realize that I do not
> have the proper
> reverent attitude.
>
> ~ Pat Wagner

The Art of Telling Digital Stories

- Joe Lambert, J. (2002). *Digital Storytelling: Capturing Lives, Capturing Community*. Berkley: Digital Diner Press.

- Seven Elements of Storytelling Tutorial (www.storycenter.org/memvoice/pages/tutorial_1.html)

Big Ideas to Ponder

- Angles Arrien's Wisdom Tales (www.angelesarrien.com/)

- Buck Minster Fuller's Quotes and Thinking (www.bfi.org/)

- Gaudiani, C. (1998). "Wisdom as Capital in Prosperous Communities." The Community of the Future. Drucker Future Foundation Series, Jossey-Bass.

- Claire L. Gaudiani's "The Wisdom Tradition:" (www.genusresources.com/site/content/publications/articles/gaudiani_wisdomtradition.asp)

- Eric Havelock's "Plato and the Transition From Orality to Literacy." (www.mcluhan.utoronto.ca/tsc_havelock_orality_literacy.htm)

- John Eisenburg's "Technology and Human Thought." (www.mcluhan.utoronto.ca/tsc_eisenberg_thought.htm)

- Marshall McLuhan's Quotes and Thinking (www.marshallmcluhan.com/)

- Parent's TV-Turnoff Reports and Resources (www.tvturnoff.org/index.html)

- Shank, R. (2000). *Tell Me a Story*. Northwestern University Press.

- Vimukt Shiksha's "Understanding Wisdom." (www.swaraj.org/shikshantar/vimukt_02.html#wc)

- Ong, W. (2002). *Orality and Literacy: The Technologizing of the Word*. Taylor & Francis Inc.

Copyright Savvy Resources

- David Warlick's Citation Machine (www.landmark-project.com)
- Hall Davidson's Copyright Quiz
  (http://halldavidson.net/downloads.html)
- Hall Davidson's Educator's Copyright Chart for Using Digital Media
  (http://halldavidson.net/downloads.html)
- David Warlick's Permission Form Templates (www.landmark-project.com)
- Stanford's University Fair Use Libraries (http://fairuse.stanford.edu)

Personal libraries function as self-portraits.

~ Al Lehmann

Digital Storytelling Websites

- Capturing Wales (www.bbc.co.uk/wales/capturewales)
- Community Building Stories (www.creativenarrations.net)
- CHYME (www.cctvcambridge.org/stream/qt/chyme)
- DigiTales StoryKeeper's Gallery (www.digitales.us)
- George Lucas Education Foundation (GLEF) (www.glef.org)
- Island Movies (Student Stories) (www.islandmovie.k12.hi.us)
- Next Exit (Dana Achtley)
  (www.nextexit.com/nextexit/showframeset.html)
- Stories of Service (Students Working with Communities)
  (www.stories-of-service.org/theproject/)
- Story Link: An Online Community (www.storylink.org)
- Telling LIVES (www.bbc.co.uk/tellinglives)
- The Center for Digital Storytelling (www.storycenter.org)
- Third World Majority (TWM) (www.cultureisaweapon.org)

A classic is a book which people praise and don't read.

~ Samuel Clemens

Evaluating Digital Products

- Online Scoring Guides for Digital Media Products: Choose "Evaluating" to use scoring guides. (www.digitales.us)

- Peer Review Processes for Reflecting on Digital Media Products: Choose "Evaluating" to see Peer Review Process. (www.digitales.us)

- Porter, B. (2000) *Evaluating Digital Products: Resource and Training Tools for Using Digital Media Scoring Guides.* www.bjpconsulting.com

- Filmmaking Rubric (www.nisd.net/cmptecww/DeptWebSite/AdvCompTech/Rubrics/Video%20Production%20Rubric.html)

Filmmaking

After the taking of Carthage, the Roman senate rewarded the family of Regulus with the books found in the city. A library was a national gift, and the most honorable they could bestow.

~ Issac Disraeli

- The Grammar of TV and Films (www.aber.ac.uk/media/Documents/short/gramtv.html)

- Theodosakis, N. (2001). *The Director in the Classroom: How Filmmaking Inspires Learning.* San Diego, Tech4Learning.

- The Making of a Thirty-second Candidate (www.pbs.org/30secondcandidate/tricks_of_the_trade/)

- Video Production Tips (www.apple.com/education/ilife/howto/imovie_tips)

Free Software Downloads

- *Atomic Learning's* Electronic Storyboard. (www.atomiclearning.com/freestoryboard.shtml)

- *Audacity Sound Editor* (http://audacity.sourceforge.net)

- *Blue Armadillo's* batch image conversion utility (Mac and WIN) (www.tech4learning.com/snacks/barmadillo.html)

- *eZedia's* Special Effects Plug-in Samplers for iMovie. (www.ezedia.com/products/downloads/)
- *Gee Three Slick's* Transition Samplers for iMovie. (www.geethree.com/)
- *ImageBlender's* 30 Day Full Version Demo. (www.tech4learning.com)
- *Inspiration's* 30 Day Full Version Demo (www.inspiration.com)
- *iTunes* (MAC and WIN) (www.apple.com/itunes/download/)
- *Photoshop Album Starter Edition* (WIN) (www.adobe.com/products/photoshopalbum/starter.htm)
- *QuickTime* (MAC and WIN) (www.apple.com/quicktime)
- *Morphing Software* (WIN) (www.morphussoftware.net)
- *Smart Sound's* (MAC and WIN) 30 Day Full Version Demo. (www.smartsound.com)
- *Windows Movie Maker 2* (WIN) (www.microsoft.com/windowsxp/moviemaker/downloads/moviemaker2.asp)

Fun Animation Stories

- Milko Cow Aerobics (http://farfar.2038.com/cow2/english/index.html)
- Harmonizing Horses (http://svt.se/hogafflahage/hogafflaHage_site/Kor/hestekor.swf)
- Mona Lisa Lip Sync (www.citesciences.fr/english/ala_cite/expo/explora/image/mona.html)
- Visual Road Education for Italians (www2.omnitel.net/smirlis/tmp/schule.html)

Future Vision Books

- Barker, J. (1992). *Future Edge*. William Morrow.

I wish there was a knob on the TV to turn up the intelligence. There's a knob called 'brightness', but it doesn't work.

~ Gallagher

When you sell a man a book, you don't sell him 12 ounces of paper and ink and glue—you sell him a whole new life.

~ Christopher Morley

- Polak, F. (1973). *The Image of the Future.* Elsevier Science.
- Schwartz, P. (1991). *The Art of the Long View.* Doubleday Currency.
- Gladwell, Malcolm. (2002). *The Tipping Point: How Little Things Can Make a Big Difference.* Little, Brown and Company.

> A book isn't born until someone reads it.
>
> ~ Christopher Morley

Getting the Writing Spirit

- Cameron, J. (1992). *The Artist's Way: A Course in Discovering and Recovering Your Creative Self.* New York, G.P. Putnam's Sons.
- Stillman, P. (1989). *Families Writing.* Writer's Digest Books.
- Ueland, B. (1987). *If You Want to Write.* Saint Paul: Graywold Press.

Good News Story Websites

- Hope Magazine (www.hopemag.com)
- Secret Society of Happy People (www.sohp.com)

> Nurture your mind with great thoughts.
>
> ~ Benjamin Disraeli

Hyper-Adventure Story Websites

- Choose-Your-Own-Adventure's Generator (Private and public story rooms available). (www.choose-your-own-adventure.com)
- HeroQuest (www.digifort.com/heroquest/)
- Multimedia Mystery (http://library.thinkquest.org/J002344/multimedia.html)
- NeverEnding Tales (www.coder.com/creations/tale/)
- The Diary of Samuel Pepys (HyperStory Read Only) (www.pepysdiary.com/)
- The Story Sprawl (www.storysprawl.com/)

Information Literacy

- Armstrong, S. (2004). *Information Literacy*. Teacher Created Materials.
- Large, P. (1984). *The Micro Revolution Revisited*. Rowman & Littlefield.
- Wurman, R. (1989). *Information Anxiety*. New York, DoubleDay.
- Wurman, R. (2001). *Information Anxiety2*. Indianapolis, Que.

Never judge a book by its movie.

~ J. W. Eagan

Learning in the 21st Century

- General National Standards Link Site by State and Subject (http://edStandards.org/Standards.html)
- Learning a Living (Skills for High Performance Workplaces) (http://wdr.doleta.gov/SCANS/lal/)
- National Standards for Storytelling (www.turnerlearning.com/turner-south/storytelling/standards.html)
- National Education Technology Standards (NETS) (www.iste.org/standards)
- North Central Regional Education Lab (NCREL)'s 21st Century Skills (www.ncrel.org/engauge/skills/21skills.htm)
- Secretary's Commission on Achieving Necessary Skills (SCANS) (http://wdr.doleta.gov/SCANS/)

There's many a bestseller that could have been prevented by a good teacher.

~ Flannery O'Connor

Learning Styles

- Armstrong, T. (1987). *In Their Own Way*. Los Angles, Tarcher. (www.thomasarmstrong.com/)
- Buzan, T. (1983). *Using Both Sides of Your Brain*. New York, Dutton.
- DePorter, B. (1992). *Quantum Learning*. New York, Dell Publishing.
- Gardner, H. (1983). *Frames of Mind*. New York: BasicBooks.

Some books are meant to be tasted, others to be swallowed, and some few to be chewed and digested.

~ Francis Bacon

Book: what they make a movie out of for television.

~ Oscar Levant

I took a speed reading course and read War and Peace in twenty minutes. It was about Russia.

~ Woody Allen

Readers are plentiful: thinkers are rare.

~ Harriet Martineau

- Jensen, E. (2001). *Arts with the Brain in Mind.* ASCD.
- Learning to Learn (Free Course) (http://adulted.about.com/gi/dynamic/offsite.htm?site=http://snow.utoronto.ca/Learn2/mod3/miinventory.html)
- Learning Styles Website Index (www.support4learning.org.uk/education/lstyles.htm)
- Left Brain/Right Brain Functions (www.viewzone.com/bicam.html)
- Levin, M. (2003). *A Mind at a Time.* New York, Simon and Schuster.
- Levine, M. (2003). *The Myth of Laziness.* New York, Simon and Schuster.
- Ornstein, R. (1986). *Multimind.* Boston, Houghton Mifflin Company.
- Multiple Intelligences online test (www.ldrc.ca/projects/miinventory/miinventory.php)
- VARK Learning Styles (www.vark-learn.com/english/index.asp)

New Science Books

- Sheldrake D. (1995). *A New Science of Life.* Inner Traditions Intl Ltd.
- Wheatley, M. (1992). *Leadership and the New Science.* San Francisco, Berrett-Koehler.

Organizational Storytelling Websites

- Corporate Storytelling Sites (www.dstory.com/dsf6/links.html#Corporate)
- Steven Denning's Organizational Storytelling (www.stevedenning.com/index.htm)
- StoryWork's Institute: Story - The Missing Piece of Your Company's Identity (www.storywork.com)

Organizational Storytelling Books

- Armstrong, D. (1992). *Managing by Storying Around: A New Method of Leadership.* Doubleday Currency.

- Denning, S. (2004). *Squirrel Inc.: A Fable of Leadership through Storytelling.* Jossey-Bass.

- Denning, S. (2001). *The Springboard: How Storytelling Ignites Action in Knowledge-Era Organizations.* Butterworth-Heinermann.

- Gabriel, Y. (2000). *Storytelling in Organizations.* New York, Oxford University Press.

Storytelling Associations and Resources

- Digital Storytelling Association (www.dsaweb.org/)

- Digital Storytelling Conference (www.dstory.com/dsfsedona/)

- National Storytelling Network (www.storynet.org/)

- StoryCon's Summit on Art, Science and the Application of Story (www.storycon.org/introToStory.htm)

- Storyteller.Net (www.storyteller.net/)

Storytelling Books

- Benjamin, W. (1969). *Iluminations.* Schocken Books

- Baur, S. (1995). *Confiding: A Psychotherapist and Her Patients Search for Stories to Live By.* Harperperennial Library.

- Collins, R. and Cooper, P. (1997) *The Power of Story: Teaching Through Storytelling.* Allyn and Bacon.

- Davis, D. (1993). *Telling Your Own Stories.* August House.

- Lankton, C and Lankton, S. (1989). *Tales of Enchantment.* New York, Brunner/Mazel.

To buy books would be a good thing if we also could buy the time to read them.

~ Arthur Schopenhauer

More information has been produced in the last 30 years than the last 5000

~ Peter Large

The saddest aspect of life right now is that science gathers knowledge faster than society gathers wisdom.

~ Isaac Asimov

- Lipman, D. (1999). *Improving Your Storytelling: Beyond the Basics for All Who Tell Stories in Work or Play*. August House.
- MaGuire, J. (1998). *The Power of Personal Storytelling: Spinning Tales to Connect with Others*. New York, Tarcher/Putnam.
- McDrury, J. and Alterio, A. (2002) *Learning Through Storytelling in Higher Education*. Kogen Page.
- Roemer, M. (1995). *Telling Stories*. Rowman & Littlefield.
- Sawyer, R. (1970). *The Way of the Storyteller*. New York, Penguin Books.
- Simmons, A. (2001). *The Story Factor: Inspiration, Influence, and Persuasion Through the Art of Storytelling*. Cambridge, Basic Books.
- Stone, E. (1989). **Black Sheep and Kissing Cousins: How Our Family Stories Shape Us**. Penguin.

Storytelling Websites

- August House (www.augusthouse.com/tell_your_story/)
- Bubbe's Back Porch (www.bubbe.com)
- Call of Story (www.callofstory.org)
- Ghost Stories (www.themoomlightroad.com)
- Learning Through Storytelling (Turner/South) (www.turnerlearning.com/turnersouth/storytelling/index.html)
- Regret to Inform (www.regrettoinform.org//flash4page.html)
- Tim Sheppard's Storytelling (www.timsheppard.co.uk/)
- Willy Claflin (www.willyclaflin.com/)

What information consumes is rather obvious: it consumes the attention of its recipients. Hence a wealth of information creates a poverty of attention, and a need to allocate that attention efficiently among the overabundance of information sources that might consume it.

~ Herbert Simon

Everybody gets so much information all day long that they lose their common sense.

~ Gertrude Stein

Technology Learning Resources

- Adobe Creative Team. (2001). *Adobe Premiere 6.0: Classroom in a Book*. Adobe Press.

- *Adobe Premiere* Interactive Videos (www.premieresecrets.com)

- Apple's *iLife* (www.apple.com/education/ilife/howto)

- *Atomic's* Online Learning Videos (For ALL products mentioned in this book) (www.atomiclearning.com)

- Heid, J. (2004). *The Macintosh iLife (w/ DVD)*. Peachpit Press.

- Digital Editing Curriculum: (www.digitalclassroom.tv/index.php?file_name= digital_video_editing_curriculum.html)

- Lee, L. (2003). *How to Use Adobe Photoshop Elements 2*. QUE.

- Levine, B. (2002). *The little iDVD Book*. Peachpit Press.

- *MovieMaker* Tutorial (www.microsoft.com/windowsxp/wmx/howto/video_wqatch.asx)

- Ozer, J. (2004). *Pinnacle Studio 9 for Windows: Visual QuickStart Guide*. Peachpit Press.

- Sadun, E. (2002). *iMovie Solutions: Tips, Tricks, and Special Effects*. Sybex.

- Storyboarding Tutorial w/videoclips. (www.storylink.org/DigitalStorytellingTool-delivery/produce_lessons.html)

- Tech4Learning's Product Tutorials (www.tech4learning.com)

- Wolsky, T. (2003). *Final Cut Express Editing Workshop (w/DVD)*. CMP Books.

You affect the world by what you browse.

~ Tim Berners-Lee

The fog of information can drive out knowledge.

~ Daniel J. Boorstin

If you believe everything you read, better not read.

~ Japanese proverb

> All of the books in the world contain no more information than is broadcast as video in a single large American city in a single year. Not all bits have equal value.
>
> ~ Carl Sagan

Technical Websites

- Digital Cameras Tips (www.tech4learning.com/snacks/dcameras.html)
- Gathering Web Resources (http://myt4l.com/index.php?page_ac=view&type=tutorials&ref_id=11)
- Keith Lightbody's Digital Video in Education (http://members.ozemail.com.au/~leemshs/digvideo.htm)
- Scanning 101 (www.scantips.com)/
- Streaming Video (http://etvcookbook.org/pc_dinners/streaming.html)
- Quicktime vs Media Player Forum (www.uemforums.com/2pop/ubbthreads/printthread.php?Cat=&Board=CleanerQuickTimeandotherCompressionApplications&main=7895&type=thread)
- United Entertainment Media Forums for Ideas, Issues and Product Comparison (www.uemforums.com/2pop/ubbthreads/ubbthreads.php?Cat=)

Visual Literacy Resources

- Burmark, L. (2002). *Visual Literacy: Learn to See, See to Learn.* ASCD.
- White, M. A. (1988). "The Third Learning Revolution," Electronic Learning, Jan. 1988.
- Lindstrom, R. (1999) "Being Visual: The Emerging Visual Enterprise." Business Week, April. 1999.
- Online 3M Meeting Guide. "Polishing Your Presentations" (www.3m.com/meetingnetwork/readingroom/meetingguide-pres.html)
- Virtual Reality Tour of Lost Cities – Peru (www.destination360.com/start1.htm)
- Visualization for Education (www.edcenter.sdsu.edu/visualize-education/)

A conclusion is simply the place where someone got tired of thinking.

~ Arthur Block